EXCUSE ME,
YOUR GOD
IS WAITING

EXCUSE ME, YOUR GOD is WAITING

LOVE YOUR GOD
CREATE YOUR LIFE
FIND YOUR TRUE SELF

MICHELLE EPIPHANY PROSSER

HAMPTON ROADS
PUBLISHING COMPANY, INC.

Cover design by Frame25 Productions
Cover art: *The Voyage* by Lee Lawson © 2006
Foreword by John St.Augustine © 2008

Hampton Roads Publishing Company, Inc.
1125 Stoney Ridge Road
Charlottesville, VA 22902
434-296-2772
fax: 434-296-5096
e-mail: hrpc@hrpub.com
www.hrpub.com

If you are unable to order this book from your local
bookseller, you may order directly from the publisher.
Call 1-800-766-8009, toll-free.

Library of Congress Cataloging-in-Publication Data

Prosser, Michelle, 1962-
  Excuse me, your God is waiting : love your God, create your life,
find your true self / Michelle Prosser.
     p. cm.
  Includes bibliographical references.
  Summary: "Through her own personal journey, the author teaches
people how to connect and converse with God. Exercises and guided
meditations throughout"--Provided by publisher.
  ISBN 978-1-57174-552-1 (pbk. : alk. paper)
  1. Spiritual life. I. Title.
  BL624.P763 2008
  204'.4--dc22
                                              2008000813

ISBN 978-1-57174-552-1

10 9 8 7 6 5 4 3 2 1

Printed on acid-free paper in Canada

Dedication

*To my father, Dr. Michael H. Prosser, a wonderful teacher
and my greatest supporter since the day I was born.*

*And to my spiritual teacher, Deane Shanks,
who has been like another father to me.*

Contents

Church of Logic • Cut Off Your Head • The Titanic of Doubt • The Many Feelings of God Are Like the Many Faces of God

See the Miracle • The Angel on Your Shoulder • Expect God's Compassion • Expect That God Is with You • It's Up to You

Refusing to Receive • Blocked by Beliefs • A Personal Relationship with God • Handling Snakes • Spiritual Hunger • Spiritual Nourishment • Splitting Ourselves • Trusting God's Voice • Feeling the Voice of God • Resisting the Feeling of God • Will I Lose Me? • Divine Union through Sex • Surrendering to God • Receiving Is about Surrendering

PART TWO CREATE YOUR LIFE WITH GOD

Put Your Toe in the Water • Adding God to Every Equation • Reconnecting with God • Take Baby Steps • A Joyful Noise • Quieting Down • Mystic Silence in Modern Times • Prayer • Decrees and Centering Prayer • Prayer Can Dance through Your Day • Prayers for Thanks • Prayers and Whitewater • Starting Your Day with Protection • Prayer as Power • Contemplation • Meditation • Chattering Monkeys • Opening Your Heart • The Practice of Samyama • Say Yes with Your Heart

Talking the Talk, Walking the Walk • Why Would God Talk to Me? • Fear of Change • Step Slowly but Surely • Stretching toward God • My Conversation with God • Accepting That God Is There • Accepting That God Is Everywhere • Believing That God Can Speak to You • Claiming Your Right to Partake of Divine Communion

A Direct Channel • Receiving YOUR Guidance from God • Rock-a My Soul • Step by Step • A Big "Aha" • Simple but Not Always Easy • Divine Communion Is a River That Quenches Your Thirst

Foreword

I slowly trudged north on the rebound side of my walk from upper Michigan to Chicago and back.[1] It was clear to me as I walked down the barren, windswept, and very cold highway that for the first time in my life I had begun to feel that I was not alone. Certainly, at times on the walk, I was surrounded by the push and pull of people hurrying off to jobs they really didn't like or appointments they had to keep but perhaps had forgotten why. But as my journey moved me further from the chaos we call society, a strange reassurance came over me, as if I was being guided by my own GPS system from within. My senses reeled and I could hear more sharply, see clearer, and feel the natural world around me as if I were an integral part of it. In short, I cannot ever remembering feeling as much alive as I did on my trek in 1996, and I know that the source of that "aliveness" is what this book is all about.

While linguists and historians debate about the origin of the word "God" (the closest they can get to the root of the modern day word *God* is the Sanskrit word *hu*, which means "to call, invoke, implore, or call upon") and the rest of humanity battles to define God and the Supreme Being's place in their lives, religion, or sporting events, it has become clear to me that the best place to find the imprint of the Almighty is within. The challenge, of course, is getting free from the diversions and distractions and being clear enough to first consider the possibility that "God is a Spirit and those that

---

[1]At the lowest point in his life, John St.Augustine undertook a miraculous journey. In an effort to raise money for the children of his community, he walked from Michigan to Chicago and back! This journey of a thousand miles became a journey of discovery, a chance for St.Augustine, whose business ventures had failed, to reinvent himself. It was on this walk that the idea for a radio show came to him; a show that would be a positive voice in a world saturated with cynicism and negativity. That started a career that led to a daily show for ten award winning years and five thousand guests from all walks of life.

come to him must come in truth and in spirit" and then trust enough to act on the beckoning of "the still, small voice."

The two concepts presented above changed my life in a dramatic fashion as I made my way north just twelve years ago. During the chaotic six months that preceded the walk, I had a short dream that repeated itself countless times, and it was always the same scene. There I was walking on the side of the road with a backpack on, near a stand of pines, with a walking stick in one hand, and the sun setting off to my left.

The dream confused me, as I was not ready to consider the source it might be coming from or the meaning it held for me. Oftentimes, the messages of God come in ways that are hidden in plain sight, and because we are so programmed to look at the whole puzzle, we often miss the pieces that create the final scene.

On a late afternoon in November, just outside a small Wisconsin town, I was in a hurry to meet a friend that I would stay with for the night. As I was focused on making my appointed pickup on time, I moved with quick steps in the fading light so as not to be walking in the dark. Rounding a curve in the road, I stepped from the blacktop to the sandy shoulder and immediately froze in my tracks. The sun was setting on my left, and on my right was a stand of seven pine trees bathed in the glow of the fading sun. "This cannot be real," my rational mind thought, but somehow I knew that I was right on course and right on time. I was standing in the scene that had been shown to me repeatedly as a preview of a coming event. At that moment, a part of me died—the small, petty ego which, of course, stands for "edging God out"—and what took its place was the GPS, or "God Possibility System." As I took one small step forward, the still small voice within, now fully connected to its host, spoke in my mind: "John, go on the radio." While the suggestion seemed out of the box at the time, the Big G had things well in hand. Less than one year later I was on the radio and, as they say, the rest is history—or "his-story."

That was the beginning of a new way of being and the way that God works through me. I surrendered my life to that which is and let go of what no longer was. With a microphone in front of me, I became a voice for purpose, possibility, and peace. In a talk radio arena, filled with people who know everything about everything but haven't done anything, the messages given to me from within found their way into people's lives and in their hearts, keeping the spark of spirit alive for at least three hours a day. I was able to speak from a place of knowing God, which is much different from knowing *of* God or believing *in* God.

That might be why you bought this book that Michelle has so lovingly and artfully co-created with that which lives in her. Most likely you are tired of the same old messages of God, as the great decider of who wins wars, football games, or elections. You might be drawn to this work because the truth that it contains is like a bright light in a darkening world and you need just a little reminder that God "lives in all, above all, and through all things," including you. Maybe you picked up this work because of the title, *Excuse Me, Your God Is Waiting,* because, truth be told, God is waiting on you and has been showing you little puzzle pieces for a long time, attempting to divert your attention away from the outer to the inner. In other words, "and be not conformed to this world: but be ye transformed by the renewing of your mind, that ye may prove what is that good, and acceptable, and perfect, will of God." It's quite possible you have been too afraid to see the signs that beckon and might have tried to drown them out with too much time on a bar stool or explain them away as "coincidences." Perhaps you don't feel worthy of God's will taking the place of your own because it pushes the envelope of trust, but whatever the reason is, what matters most is this book is now in your hands.

Michelle has given birth to a real gift—the concepts, thoughts, and stories presented are representations of what happens when you become the conduit for Spirit, and are willing to be a messenger for the greatest message of our times . . . that God is alive in you and has only one small request to guide your life—that is to simply listen within and trust the process. There is a lot of talk from people that "found God" as if the all-knowing, all-being architect of the universe has been somehow playing a cosmic game of hide and seek with humanity since the dawn of time. I rather like to think that as I wandered down that bone chilling country road looking for myself— God found me—for it is we who are lost and searching for home, not the other way around. A pretty smart carpenter once said a long time ago: "Of myself I can do nothing, but the Father that dwells within me, he does the work." Thanks to Michelle and *Excuse Me, Your God Is Waiting,* it's now your turn to "be a light unto the world." On behalf of the rest of humanity, thanks for answering the call.

—John St.Augustine,
producer
Oprah & Friends

A river runs through these pages, like it runs through our lives. We don't have a choice of whether or not we are in this river. What we do have a choice about is whether we struggle against it, try to push it along, or surrender to its current and go downstream. We have a choice to approach our life with joy, with playfulness, with power, and with love. We can fight the river or turn and flow with the current.

Images of rivers have always run through my life. I had images of drowning when I was a teenager and my parents divorced. As one career success after another occurred in my twenties and thirties, I felt like I was riding a river current.

When my children arrived as miracles in my life, I knew I was in a river filled with grace.

Finally, when I went to a women's shelter for counseling because of my marriage, I told my therapist I was having dreams and visions of myself struggling to wade upstream in a river, fighting the current. As I went through my divorce, there were times when I felt like I was barely keeping my head above water.

I am drawn to rivers. I have swum, canoed, and floated lazily in an inner tube down rivers. With my heart beating wildly, I have ridden a raft in Class V rapids. The metaphor of rivers shows up in my coaching. I urge clients to see that they have a choice in their lives. They can view themselves as dog-paddling in the river, struggling to keep their head above water, or they can choose to be the navigator of their own boat. Either way, they are on the water, experiencing both the gentle flow of the river and rough water, rocks, and storms. To be in the river, caught up in the current and in danger of drowning, is to be a victim. As a navigator in life, we take back our power and make choices regardless of what the river throws at us. And always, we can decide to play with the river or fight it.

It is my hope that what is contained in these pages will help you navigate the river of your life with joy and ease. And that you can live your life by going downstream, not upstream against the current.

I only have one request as we start out on this leg of the journey: Fill your boat with joy and playfulness as you push it into the water.

God Speaks to the Soul

And God said to the soul:
I desired you before the world began.
I desire you now
As you desire me.
And where the desires of two come together
There love is perfected.

—Mechthild of Magdeburg, medieval mystic

My soul has always been searching.

As a spiritual seeker, I've invested a few decades learning from a wonderful array of wise teachers. As a corporate and life success coach, I've spent years teaching people how to be successful and I have a whole toolbox of techniques to help them. But the story you will read here paints a different picture of me as I faced crisis after crisis before I was able to clearly hear God's guidance. I'll share how I have slowly come to clearly hear God, allowed God into my life, and received the love so freely given.

As I reread these pages, I feel naked—so vulnerable that perhaps you can see some of me in you. I share my joys and triumphs, my follies and mistakes, my grief and heartaches. Naked is what we are with our Source, our Creator, who sees all and embraces everything we are. There is no hiding from God, so I choose not to hide from you.

The Searching of Your Soul

We cannot hide from God's desire to love and connect with us either, although many of us choose not to hear the whispers that come to us in mystical moments. Every day we have the opportunity to be a mystic. To be a mystic means one has "intimate union" with the Divine. Mystics do not only exist in monasteries or ashrams, nor did they only live in medieval times. Each of us has the ability to be a modern mystic—to yield to the longing of our souls and to feel God speak to us moment to moment.

All of us have souls that are searching—yearning for Divine connection —whether we want to admit it or not. This is why we feel such discontent. Bliss arises when we surrender to our longing and embrace our inner mystic.

God speaks to us all the time, in many ways. Today you hold an invitation in your hands to reach your Divine potential. This invitation comes *through* me, not *from* me. It is issued in my handwriting, but it does not bear my return address. Stamped, sealed, and delivered to you, it invites you to live a life of power and magnificence as the radiant being you are.

It is your choice whether you accept this invitation. The caveat is that your life will change, as my life has changed. Come join me on this journey, riding the river of life. Here I share my travels with you so that your way may be smoother.

Going Back to Your Source

Sometimes we can feel the calling of our soul, but we need others to help us find our way back home. Traditionally, clergy and elders served this role, but today choices include coaches, therapists, and alternative healers, among others. I coach clients working in corporations, government, law firms, educational organizations, and nonprofits. Inevitably we discuss where energy originates and how positive energy creates success. We must all go back to the beginning—our Source.

Looking for our Source takes us to God, even if we dance around that topic. People are so hungry for that connection—whether or not they feel comfortable talking about it in traditional religious terms.

When clients are confused or despondent, I counsel them to ask God for guidance in their lives. When they are faced with a crisis or feel threatened, I share with them prayers for protection. When they are in pain, I suggest they ask for healing. When they want to manifest successful outcomes, I teach them how to ask God for what they want and cocreate that life. I seldom use the name "God" or the word "prayer." Yet I usually find myself coaching clients about how to have a conversation with their personal God.

I do not see myself as a missionary to corporate America. I never walk into someone's office with the intent of teaching prayer. I did not start out my coaching career as a spiritual teacher, although my spiritual path did lead me to coaching. I have a deep desire to help people become more successful, focused, balanced, and fulfilled. And in doing so, I have become known as a corporate mystic.

Before becoming a coach, I spent twenty years as a political junkie, working in politics and government, a life in which it was difficult to find balance. It was a life so consuming that it was easy to lose sight of what I valued most. I held leadership positions with three governors and a congressman, as well as in several statewide campaigns. To steady myself, I slowly returned to a deep connection with my Source. Eventually, I became brave enough to share this with people I worked with to help them keep their footing despite the consuming demands of political life.

At the end of my political career, I was leading guided meditations with candidates before they went on stage. I was praying with them for guidance about major decisions. This might not seem unusual for conservative politicians who tend to be vocal about God, but I worked with progressive, liberal leaders. I discovered that most people, regardless of their ideology or religious background, are hungry to find their way back to God.

As the fourth-century Saint Augustine wrote, "*My soul cannot rest until it rests in thee, my God.*"

Hungry for God

Because I, too, was hungry for God, I started a personal quest for Her in my life and found my own path toward joy and love. Two books profoundly influenced my life. The first was *Conversations with God,* by Neale Donald Walsch, which helped me learn to ask God for what I want and to realize that I create my life through my thoughts and feelings. This book helped me deepen my own personal conversation with God. The second book was *Excuse Me, Your Life Is Waiting,* by Lynn Grabhorn, which simplified the Law of Attraction. I have incorporated concepts from both books into the way I live and into what I teach my coaching clients.

These two books shifted my life view and the relationship I forge with God. I moved from a victim perspective, as an insecure daughter, grieving mother, abused wife, and struggling single mother, into accepting my true power and beauty. I made the decision to honor God by honoring myself and creating a life that was worthy of the gift I had been given. My direct connection with God changes my life every day.

Rivers Flow

As I wrote this book, rivers kept coming to me. The goals poster I made for myself was filled with pictures of flowing water. I prayed that my writing would flow like water, easefully, so that I might help others. One day I realized that what I really needed was a simple cabin where I could retreat from my busy life and complete my book. In less than a month, the offer of a cabin, which sat in front of two streams that flowed into a river, appeared. (Yes, miracles do exist!)

Everywhere I turned, teachers were speaking about water, from the *Tao Te Ching* to the Holy Bible and Zen writings. Two teachers who have influenced me greatly—Esther and Jerry Hicks and their channeled teachings of Abraham—powerfully use the metaphor of the river.

A Compass and a Map

We cannot travel on water without tools to help us orient ourselves. While writing this book, an orienteer came into my life. An expert at helping people find their way through dense forests, he showed me how to use a compass and a map. He is also the one who lent me the cabin, so I could find myself.

With the quiet, I started to see my life as a map—of where I had been and where I was headed. Sometimes I worried that I had been traveling in circles, like the way a whirlpool turns a leaf on the surface of a river. Instead, I realized I *had* traveled quite a distance and even in those times when I felt I was in a circle, it was a spiral that helped my focus grow tighter as I grew.

Our thoughts and feelings are our internal compass. In the movie *Pirates of the Caribbean,* a magic compass points toward what one truly wants. Like that compass, I realized that my soul's deepest desires can point me to where I need to go. If I let my thoughts and feelings spin wildly around like a compass that gets too close to a magnet, I am thrown off my mark. Yet if I can pause and reset my compass to true north—my Source—I know how to orient myself. It is my wish that you, too, can discover your map and reset your compass so your life journey will be informed by self-knowing and your soul's direction.

Are You Ready?

Excuse Me, Your God Is Waiting is for those who want to see God in a different way, hear God for themselves, and create a joyful life that supports them in living their Divine potential.

God is God. Let's discover an image of God that you can invite into your life. We will unearth our beliefs about a God we don't want and allow our resistance to God, built upon these beliefs, to dissolve. We can create God in the likeness we want and then feel God's presence. In doing so, we can move toward expecting His constant presence, listening to His voice, and allowing God into our lives in a deeper, more personal way.

You will notice that I choose to use both male and female gender pronouns when writing about God. I hope you will be comfortable or become comfortable with thinking of God as beyond gender characterization, so you, too, can picture your God in the most loving, compassionate way you choose. In addition, I come from a Christian perspective, although I find inspiration from varied spiritual traditions that are not Christian. If possible, try to see beyond my perspective to find the God you want.

The first section of this book will help you identify the God you want so you can move past old barriers and truly love and receive your God. The second section teaches you to share direct communion with your God so that you can cocreate your life in Divine partnership. The third section guides you in become consciously empowered as you find your true self and in making better choices while you cocreate a life of joyful significance by partnering with God.

Through exercises and meditations, together we will discover a God with whom you can connect and, conversely, a God you can understand. You may have written God out of your life, you may have made some tentative steps, or you may already have a relationship and want to deepen it—all situations can benefit from this journey. You will also discover your true self, for in knowing yourself, you know God more deeply.

Wake Up and Change Your Life

This will change your life if you are ready for it. The big question is: Are you ready for it?

Are you *really* ready for it?

I invite you to wake up. Wake up to a life full of love, joy, meaning, fulfillment, and power. Wake up to the deepest relationship of your life. Wake up to healing so you can receive. God is waiting for you. It is time to partake of Divine communion.

PART ONE

Love Your God

CHAPTER 1

Excuse Me

My river of life flows with God's grace. As I catch the current each day, I feel God guiding me in the right direction. When I follow this guidance, abundant gifts fill my life like smooth river rocks lining the banks.

Miracles are everywhere.

My beautiful children came to me despite fertility problems. Our home is the house we desired. I realized my life's calling and was able to create my own business. I travel the world. I am gifted with friendships that are substantial and rewarding.

I decided I wanted to write a book to share these blessings and held it as an intention without taking any action. One day a publisher arrived as a coaching client and later requested I write a book for his company.

Every day, miracles appear and I am finally centered enough to see them. Butterflies pause on my hand. Someone gives me a book that inspires an "aha" moment. I hear my children giggle.

Life has not always been this way for me. Often I fought the current, swimming upstream, or tried to push the river in a direction it was not flowing. What resulted was a persistent run of life crises that kept knocking me to my knees. One after another, they swept over me, wedging me between sharp rocks and pounding me into a person I didn't want to be. My life changed when I realized that, on some level, I felt like I deserved these disasters.

I came to understand that I, Michelle Epiphany Prosser, who coached her clients to love, believe in, and honor themselves, had a rip in her own heart that had not yet healed.

That ultimately, TRAGICALLY, I believed I was not worthy.
Then I realized that my God was waiting for me.
Waiting for me to reach my hand out of the rushing floodwaters
and ask for help. Waiting to help heal my wounds and guide my jour-
ney.
The good news is that my story has a happy ending and yours can,
too!

The Law of Attraction is a powerful law of the universe. In principle, it is pretty simple. Like attracts like. What we put our attention to, we attract to our lives. Our power is in our thoughts and feelings; far more power than most people realize. These thoughts and feelings allow us to create magic in our lives. Or they can pull in problems. When we use it consciously, we can create miracles. We ask for what we want, feel it coming, and receive it in.

It is the secret that many successful individuals have used throughout the ages. Now word of it is spreading like wildfire due to books like *Excuse Me, Your Life is Waiting* by Lynn Grabhorn, *You Can Heal Your Life* by Louise Hay, *Ask and It Is Given* and *The Amazing Power of Deliberate Intent* by Esther and Jerry Hicks, as well as two books by Wayne Dyer, *The Power of Intention* and *Real Magic*.

The section on the Law of Attraction in the sleeper hit film *What the Bleep Do We Know?!* generated a huge response on its website. The book *The Secret,* by Rhonda Byrne, became an overnight sensation, as did the DVD release. When several teachers from *The Secret* appeared twice on Oprah in the span of a week, the show garnered tremendous feedback. The Law of Attraction has become all the buzz.

When news of this secret reached the mainstream, I began to wonder how it fits into what we have been taught about God. Others tell me they wonder whether the Law of Attraction negates or replaces God. If we use it, are we trying to make ourselves equal to God? Where does God fit into the equation?

Many of us learned restrictive, sometimes negative beliefs about God from the institutions that are trying to draw us closer to God: our organized religions. Religious teachings often limit us from seeing our power and magnificence. This humbling idea forms an invisible energy field around us that repels what we want most.

No wonder so many people push away the image of God, considering the negative images that have been presented to us. We have been made to feel smaller, weaker, and less than we are because of what we were taught about God and about ourselves.

The truth is: The biggest stumbling block to the Law of Attraction is that *we are not allowing ourselves to receive the very things we are requesting.* The cure is to connect with God so that we can be made whole and be guided in cocreating the life we want. When God is part of the equation, the success of attracting and receiving what you really want, and becoming who you want to be, expands exponentially.

The Law of Attraction . . . and God

The Law of Attraction is always working, whether you choose to use it or not. You are manifesting what happens in your life, both good and bad. What many of us forget when we start consciously using the Law of Attraction is that we don't have to do it on our own.

After the initial rush of pulling in what we want, many of us soberly realize what being responsible for our lives really means. We start to understand that we are creating the pain in our lives, yet try as we might, we cannot live a life without pain. Some pain is required in order to learn and grow. We all need some friction, some sand in our oyster shell, to grow a pearl. To fully know joy, we need to experience sadness. We cannot know something unless we know its opposite. This is another law of the universe: the Law of Polarity, sometimes called the Law of Opposites.

Still, it can feel lonely when we realize how powerful we are in creating our lives, especially when we continue to create hardship. Instead of feeling empowered when a crisis hits because we know that we are powerful enough to move through it, we blame ourselves for doing something wrong by creating the crisis.

We struggle with the Law of Attraction when we can't seem to move through negative emotions, like fear, grief, or a sense of unworthiness, which attract further negativity, into positive emotions, which attract positive outcomes. We know *intellectually* that we need to be more positive, but we seem unable to move there emotionally.

So here is a truth about the Law of Attraction that few people know: *Even the Law of Attraction is overridden by Divine intervention.* When you are trapped in fear, doubt, anger, or grief, all you need do is ask for help. You will receive assistance so that you can move into positive energy again; you don't have to do it on your own.

I remember sharing this insight around a dinner table with friends, nationally known master manifesters who earn their living working with spiritual concepts. Each of them has created an amazing life, yet everyone paused, took a deep breath, and sighed with relief. It is easy to get so caught up in the Law of Attraction that we come to believe it is the only law in the Universe. There *are* other laws—and the greatest law is God's power. Divine intervention takes the pressure off. We do have someone else to help us.

When you dissolve your resistance to God, whether conscious or subconscious, and invite Her into your life, you can relax. You are partnered with a powerful cocreator. All of a sudden, not only can you attract magic into your life, but you can also cocreate miracles. And if you stumble and fall into fear, you always have God to help you recover.

When we add God to the equation, along with the Law of Attraction, we are so powerful that all our outcomes are successful, even when they don't seem so initially. By having earnest communion with God, we learn to trust that, even when it seems we have taken a wrong turn, we have simply discovered a new shortcut to our dreams. God takes us seriously when we ask for what we want. The New Testament says, *"Ask and you shall receive. Knock and the door shall be opened for you."* Sometimes we are simply unable to realize that we have received exactly what we requested.

Many of us harbor resistance to adding God to the Law of Attraction equation. After all, it may have taken a lifetime to feel powerful enough to learn how to use it. Why do we need to return to an entity that we have been taught makes us feel small and weak?

Missing Your Connection

Let me reframe this for you. Have you ever waited patiently for a loved one to arrive? Although you were unsure about his arrival time, you were content to wait because you knew that soon you would be together. Your heart was filled with joyful anticipation.

Perhaps as this person walked into the restaurant, or emerged from the plane, he did not see you. Maybe some time had passed since you last saw one another so he did not recognize you. When you called his name, you were too far away and he could not hear you. Until you were able to connect, both of you felt keenly disappointed because you were so eager to be together.

I am here to tell you that you have a devoted friend waiting patiently for you. Like the friendly stranger who taps you on the shoulder to alert you to your friend's call, I am here to point out your friend to you.

Maybe your eyes are not clear enough to see Her. Perhaps She does not look as you expected. Maybe there is too much noise and you are unable to hear Her as She calls your name, even though She is practically jumping up and down to catch your attention.

Excuse me, your God is waiting for you. He has been waiting patiently, yet eagerly, to connect with His old friend. God has been waiting for you to recognize Him. He wants to help you as you create a new, different life.

Can you hear God's voice? She is calling to you every day. She is longing to have you open up and embrace Her.

He has been trying to tell you how much He loves you and how magnificent and beautiful you are in His eyes. He wants to be with you as you live a joyful life full of purpose and meaning.

God Wants a Conversation with You

You may react with "Who, me?" Why would God want to talk to me? Why would I be worthy of a conversation with God?

Or why would I want to talk with God—a God who has let me down or forgotten me? Or One who is angry or vengeful and punishes Her children? Why would I want anything to do with a God whose people kill each other in Her name?

In these instances, you are viewing yourself or viewing God with a preconceived image of worthiness. You have projected a lifetime full of images, many imposed by others, onto *your* image of God. Can you set these judgments aside for a moment? Can you sit with an open mind and an open heart, regarding both yourself and your true God?

Can you hold a space of love and allow a new perspective to sprout through cracks in the wall that is holding you back from appreciating yourself and your deeper relationship with God?

Can you put aside all that you have been taught about God—all projections, fears, judgments, and prejudices? If you can let go of the images you hold about God, you will start a new, beneficial relationship. And as you do so, you may develop a new appreciation for who *you* are.

It could be that you already feel like you have a good relationship with God and you don't need to deepen it. Maybe on some level you feel resistant to getting closer, perhaps even some fear of getting too close to the Big Guy. Yet your life is not fulfilling or going the way you wanted.

How would it be to recognize clearly God within us and around us? To be able to see our worth and know what a gift we are to this world? To believe that the best gift we can give God and others is to live our own Divine potential? And to allow ourselves to claim God as ours, not as how others would have us see Her?

We are the magnificent, beautiful, powerful, and whole children of a benevolent God. Most of us are asleep to this truth. Wake, beautiful sleepers, wake to the world, wake to your blessings, wake to God's voice among you; know that you are all children of God.

God wants you to live a powerful life. God wants to cocreate with you a life full of joy, meaning, and purpose. He wants to share with you the ways you can attract what you want into your life. More than anything, God wants you to live a life that allows you to be who you really want to be. He wants you to live out your Divine potential. If you heed His guidance, you can take steps toward the life that is right for you. If you learn how to ask Him for what you want, together you can cocreate the life you crave. And if you can open to Him, you can live a life filled with a special love found nowhere else.

A Testament of Love

There is the Old Testament and the New Testament. There is the Hindu Bhagavad-Gita and the Muslim Koran. There are many religious texts that testify about God.

This book is a testament of love. Love is what is. Love is what God is. Love is what you are. When we feel love, whether for our parents, mates, children, friends, or a puppy, it is a nudge to remember ourselves and to remember God. We don't *do* love, we *are* love. When we remember this, feel love, and partner with God, we are closer to our Divine potential.

There are only two states. There is love and there is fear. Yet even in fear, love exists, for love is everywhere. Fear arises when love is forgotten. Love dwells perpetually in every cell of our body. We may not always feel the love, but it is there. It's vibrating inside us. Much like a Tibetan singing bowl, the vibration continues beyond what we can hear. We know this when we touch the metal of a singing bowl and still feel its vibration even after we can't hear the tone. Living a life of gratitude, mercy, compassion, or appreciation can raise our love vibration higher. When we raise our vibration, we change the way we live and how others live with us; it touches us even when we don't realize it.

We cannot be connected to well-being unless we feel well-being, because we get what matches our vibration. What we focus on is what we feel. What we feel is what we vibrate. What we vibrate is what we attract.

Throughout history, many have referred to the Law of Attraction as the Law of Love. Live in love and you live in abundance. If we love others, we are not burdened by negative energy. We naturally create positive energy and that energy pulls goodness to us. If we love ourselves, we can receive all the goodness that is possible.

It is simple but not easy. This book can serve as a guidebook for your personal journey.

Obtaining the Life You Want

We live the life we want not by DOING but by BEING. Be love. It is not what we do, but the energy we hold that determines our success in life.

Let me say this again:

It is not what we do, but the energy we hold that determines our success in life.

We are energy—an energetic field of vibration. It is this energy that impacts our outcomes, that creates our dreams, that colors how life feels to us. It allows for heaven here on Earth. When love infuses our vibration, our energy is like a sports drink for the soul. We become champions in our lives. We win at life.

Life does not happen *to* us. We create our lives; we pull them to us. We are the most powerful force in the Universe when we cocreate with God. When we value ourselves and celebrate the gift of life, we are rewarded. When we devalue ourselves and view life from a victim's perspective, then that is what we live. The vibration of the victim consciousness is one that quickly becomes self-fulfilling.

We define ourselves by our stories. We lug them around with us like well-packed steamer trunks. They take up much of our energy and wear us out. They limit us. In fact, we insist on squeezing ourselves into a small package labeled damaged, unworthy, or bad.

Our stories help shape us but they don't have to minimize us. Many of us have deep wounds, but we are far more resilient than we believe. Though we have made big mistakes, a bigger mistake would be to inhibit our growth because we fear a new blunder. Like a graceful tree, we grow *around* the damaged parts and reach up high toward the sun.

Don't mourn your brokenness; celebrate your wholeness. Hear the call to move past self-loathing, past self-sabotage, past the shame, the negative attitude, and the pettiness. Respond by asking for healing and for the help to love yourself and rise to your highest level.

How blessed we are! How beautiful and perfect we are, even in our brokenness. Like a child's favorite toy, we become love-worn and more desirable because of the wear. But we are not a toy; we are God's beloved children. We each possess God's nature and spark inside of us, just as children carry their parents' DNA. We are all like God, made in Her likeness, and we possess the ability to love as God loves.

The Challenge

Today, you are presented a message filled with love and hope. It requires courage to consider it. You are dared to create God in an image that allows you to establish a full, direct relationship with Him. You are dared to fully expand yourself. By receiving God, you receive your Divine inheritance.

Are you brave enough to do this, to actually live the life you want? A direct relationship with God *will* change your life. And you are now dared to recreate yourself so that you live in love.

Excuse Me, Your God Is Waiting urges a paradigm shift that permits you to find the God you want. You can converse and partner with God to create miracles in your life. You can accept God's love and return it with every cell of your being. When you do this, you access tremendous energy, wisdom, and power.

This means that you must shed the images of God that are not serving you. You are required to let go of how other people have defined God for you and go find Him yourself. This is not for the lazy or weak of heart.

We are challenged to take God outside the box that humans have constructed and open up to our own connection with our Creator. Each of us must walk uncharted territory. Without step-by-step directions, we must find our own way. But there is always a voice calling to us. God never stops talking to us. Our task is to be able to listen to Her voice. God's voice orients our compass, always pointing toward where we need to go.

How do I know this? I have taken this journey. I have my own personal conversations with God. I am just like you but I have learned to listen. I have slowly come to understand the language of God. I open to allow God into my life and receive His love. And so can you.

The world can be your oyster. You have only to give your attention to what's coming instead of what's not here. Once you are comfortable doing that, by the powers that be and the power you are, you will begin to live the life you came here to live. You will be fulfilling your reason for being.

—Lynn Grabhorn, *Excuse Me, Your Life Is Waiting,* page 305

You are goodness and mercy and compassion and understanding. You are peace and joy and light. You are forgiveness and patience, strength and courage, a helper in time of need, a comforter in time of sorrow, a healer in time of injury, a teacher in times of confusion.

You are the deepest wisdom and the highest truth; the greatest peace and the grandest love. You are these things, and in moments of your life you have known yourself as these things. Choose now to know yourself as these things always.

—Neale Donald Walsch, *Conversations with God, Book 1,* page 86

CHAPTER 2

YOUR God Is Waiting for You

I have always felt a deep love for God, a longing for connection, a thirst that could not be quenched by anything or anyone else. And yet sometimes I pushed against it from trepidation of how God had been portrayed to me. I didn't want the angry authoritarian male God with a long white beard, piercing eyes, and stern face.

There were times, as a small child, that I was afraid to go to sleep because I knew from Bible stories that God often came and spoke to people in their dreams. God asked Jonah to do things he resisted and that resistance landed him in the belly of a whale. What would God ask of me? Could I end up in the belly of a whale?

Growing up Catholic, my greatest fear was that God would come to me in my dreams and ask me to be a nun. Even as a small child I longed to be a mother and becoming a nun would ruin that surely. Though I yearned for a mystical connection with God, before I went to bed I would plead, "Don't make me be a nun for you." Then I would try to stay awake so I wouldn't have the dream in which God appeared to issue this command.

Fortunately, God has come to me in my dreams many times, and She never did ask me to be a nun. In fact, She came to announce the blessed arrival of each of my children.

It is amazing, with fears like that, that I even wanted a conversation with God! I look back at that poor child, tossing and turning in bed, afraid of talking with God. Who would want to get close to a God so scary that He rivaled a trip to the principal's office, or worse?

Many of us are like that tired child before bed, hungry for a connection but fearful of having a relationship with God. Because what might She ask of us? Would we be required to be in harm's way? What might She ask us to give up?

At some point in our lives, most of us learn that listening to God means we have to give up our heart's desire. Yet part of our heart's desire is to merge with our Creator. So, as we feel the pull toward God, we also push against moving closer.

Who told us that to love God we had to give up our dreams? What kind of God would give us such deep desires and then ask us to discard them? Who told us that God was scary and angry? Or that God had a beard? Or that He is male? Why must we feel locked into an image of God that others have imposed on us?

Identify the God You Want

The time is ripe to create your own image of God. We need a God who energizes, inspires, and partners with us for a life filled with joy. We need a joint venture that fully aligns us with God even if we already have a nodding relationship. We need an existence in which we have a deep relationship with God so we can cocreate together.

Many think they have to live life on their own. They have this bleak belief that they exist alone, separate from any Divine support. So many are hungry for a spiritual connection but cannot move past the image of the traditional God forced on them by dogmatic religions that use guilt, shame, and castigation to manipulate their congregations.

Through working with my clients, I see the many ways individuals are hurt by traditional religions. They are so wounded and angry that they reject spiritual experiences, even as they grieve the loss of spirituality in their lives. I strive to help them move past these blocks to find a God that they can invite into their lives.

You too can move past your blocks to find the right God to invite in. Make a firm stand. Refuse to allow others the power to define God for you. Claim this power as YOUR RIGHT. You decide who God is. And then, connecting with God, learn how to create your own life.

GOD'S PORTRAIT

How was God portrayed to you as a child? How about as an adult? What were you told God looks like? List the qualities you used to believe God possessed. Are they the same as what you believe now?

Identify the God You Don't Want

Lynn Grabhorn writes that the first step in the Law of Attraction is to figure out what we don't want so we can determine more clearly what we want. Take a look at the God you don't want. Even as a child I knew I did not want a stern, angry grandfather who imposed his will on me regardless of my desires.

Let go of all the images that have been imposed on you. If you have a considerable emotional charge about God, take a look at that. Many speak in the name of God, but few speak FOR God. You will know if the message is based in love and acceptance. If God's name is invoked to berate, shame, or control you, then God's name has been spoken in vain. This is not God's message. All the great teachers tell us that God is love.

Reject the messages of God that are meant to control and humble you. Identify the God you don't want. Find the portrayal of God that makes you hold back or even push away from God.

Who is the God you don't want? Even if you have already accepted a God that you want, stretch further in order to connect more deeply. Think about all the images and teachings about God you don't want to accept. That is where many people remain stuck— in their "don't wants" about God. Because of these, they block God from their hearts. We must make conscious all the reasons we hold ourselves back from connecting with God. Unconscious beliefs and judgments that we accepted a long time ago color our perspective if they remain unseen and unchallenged.

THE GOD YOU DON'T WANT

Close your eyes and feel into your heart. As if you are watching a documentary film, bring up images and statements about God that you were exposed to and notice how your body and heart reacts to these messages. What messages bring up a strong negative reaction in you? Write a list of the qualities of a God you don't want.

Move past what repels and hurts you to the God you want. Create God in the image and likeness that inspires, motivates, and creates a connection for you. If you can see God as approachable, then you can reach out and invite Him into your life. And in that moment, you change your life.

Tune out what others say about God. Later you can return to the spiritual teachers who inspire and enlighten you. But first be quiet and still. Allow yourself to feel the pull to whatever God you are able to adore. Feel the energy of your God. Listen to the whispers of your God to hear Her tell you who She is.

Who Does Your God Say He Is?

When I listen quietly, what comes to me about God is:

He is bigger than we can know. He is He and He is She, male and female energy. We are His stars in a vast endless sky. God is the sun, the moon, the space between the stars, and He resides in us, His stars. God is without a face, and yet has all our faces. God is all. God fills the nothingness.

When I hear this, it fills me with wonder and awe. It makes me feel spacious and vast in my heart. I become one with the vastness of God. This is not an image that confines, restricts, or reduces me. It is an image that expands, engages, and enlightens me.

I understand why the Sufi whirling dervishes spin around in circles until they are dizzy. I comprehend why the Shakers danced into frenzies, why the Native Americans go on Vision Quests to see the face of God. I know why Muslims face extreme danger to journey to Mecca, and why African American churches raise their voices so loudly in praise that the church walls shake. When we feel God this way, we are bigger, better, higher versions of ourselves.

OPEN YOUR MIND

Open your mind. If you were to imagine a God who could make you feel like a bigger, better, higher version of yourself, who would He be? Who does your God say He is?

Putting God in a Box

Many of us have been taught to see a God who makes us feel small, weak, and less than holy. Humans have always struggled with how to explain the unexplainable and sometimes we falter. When we cannot grasp Her in Her vastness, we try to box Her into a structure that we can understand. In doing so, we reduce Her. We project our flaws, our failings, and our smallness onto the boundless face of God.

Sometimes we try to shut the door and make believe God is not there, just like the child who, afraid of monsters, believes that closing her closet door will keep them at bay.

God is often portrayed as the ultimate parent, but for many this means a stern authority figure. We must either dread Him or obey Him.

Portraying God as a parent is a mixed bag because not all parents are created equal. People who grew up with loving, healthy parents find comfort in their image of God as a nurturing parent. For those who grew up with dysfunctional or abusive parents, the image of God as a parent stirs painful memories. Perhaps those who speak of a vengeful, angry, and punishing God had parents of this sort.

Rare are the children who have experienced complete and unconditional love from their parents. Unconditional love means *you are loved for being, not for doing.* We need not do a single thing to be loved by God. Just by the act of existing, we are loved.

Since few have experienced this, it is hard to grasp fully what this means. Instead, we compare God's love to what we know, which is based on pleasing our disapproving parents for their conditional love. Like children, we split God in two and try to name Her either as the good parent or the bad. He is the angel on our shoulder or the scary creature under the bed. We insist that we must see Her in black and white. This is why so many have distorted God's image.

Judging God by His Relatives

God has all sorts of children, some of whom are not coming from their higher selves when they teach about Him. They use His name to evoke fear. They use His teaching to feed their own egos or further an organization's power. They use God to take away people's power, not to empower them.

Religions sometimes treat their congregations as if they are children who need to be told what to do. They believe that only their leaders can interpret God's messages, and that the rest of us are incapable of having a conversation with God. God is invoked to impose their agenda, their judgments, and their rules.

Religious leaders like this are the black sheep of our human family, those who ruin God's name. Most of us have relatives who embarrass or misrepresent us. We cringe when we are linked to them. I have a family member who frequently speaks ill of me. In those moments, I fervently hope that people will judge me for me, not for how I am represented. I want people to get to know me—the REAL me—not how I have been portrayed by someone else.

If we believe that God is love, then we feel His presence all the time, every time we sense love. If God is love, then we shouldn't believe what the angry minister yells at us in church. We cannot believe the rationale a vengeful terrorist uses to justify killing innocents. We cannot believe that God's bidding is used to oppress women and abuse children. We cannot believe that He wants countries to go to war in his name. We cannot believe there is such a thing as a Holy War or Jihad.

To truly know God, we must listen to Her. When we choose to listen to others, we need to be discriminating about who speaks for Her. The polygraph test is whether they are words of love . . . or words of fear.

Religion Can Cause the Deepest Wounds

Religion's higher purpose is to guide and support us on the path to enlightenment—not to force the path. Yet many religions claim they are the only way to salvation. This, in itself, gives us a sense of separation that goes against communing with God. Instead of seeing ourselves as One, we see ourselves as separate from all, including God: separate from our brothers and sisters who choose different paths; from ourselves, because we think we are not worthy enough; and from the version of a God who is jealous, vengeful, and judgmental.

Traditional religion has engraved deep wounds in some people. Threats of fire, brimstone, or eternal damnation puncture children's original sense of their magnificence. They are taught to be less than they are and grow up as adults who believe on some deep level that they are not enough.

In working with clients, I see adults who struggle with feelings of unworthiness and who have often accepted negative messages from their religious traditions or parents. Many who grew up in fundamentalist Christian churches define themselves as unworthy sinners. Most people cannot see their inherent perfection, instead accepting the idea that they are all products of original sin.

Matthew Fox, in his book *Original Blessing,* argues that we are all born with an original blessing instead of original sin. In his work, he provides another viewpoint about the traditional fall-redemption ideology that is so pervasive in our society.

Coming from a Catholic tradition, I see how so many people suffer from guilt about their sexuality. They are so damaged that even in the comfortable confines of a marriage they are unable to accept their sexuality as a gift. Instead, they see themselves as dirty. They suppress and push away pleasure because it is a symbol of being weak and sinful.

RELIGIOUS WOUNDING

Have you been wounded by portrayals of God? Has your religious upbringing or societal messages about God made you feel less instead of more? What might these messages be? What might you do to free yourself of these negative messages?

Betrayal in God's Name

One of my clients is unwavering in her belief that God betrayed her. She grew up in an abusive home, regularly beaten by her father, and hoped that God could help her. As a young teenager, she went, in desperation, to her pastor to share her pain and ask for help. He sent her home. She arrived home to discover that the pastor had called her father to tell him what she had revealed. She suffered the worst beating of her life. In that moment, she decided that God had "set her up" and she would never again allow Him into her life. In her mind, the pastor who betrayed her represented God's betrayal.

Recently, several young girls raised in a rural Bible Belt community have come forward to accuse their pastors of rape and molestation. These children were told that it was God's will that their pastor violate them. The same message was conveyed to many young boys who were sexually abused by priests.

Young girls are told they are obeying God's command when they are forced, by fundamental polygamists, to marry an older men and become one of several wives. God's dictates are used as the justification promoting female genital mutilation in Africa and the stoning to death of female adulterers in conservative Muslim countries.

The Taliban provide the most extreme example of fundamental Muslims using God's name to inflict abuse on women, which is ironic because Mohammed's progressive views about women caused social unrest during his lifetime. Even in relatively progressive Israel, a vigilante group of Orthodox Jewish men patrol buses to force women to sit in the back.

Experiences like this cause people to cut themselves off from God, or to fear God. For some, the pain is so deep that they refuse to believe there is a God. After all, He was not there when they needed Him. They become like the badly abused teen, who, once she leaves home, cuts off all contact with her family. God is seen as a predator because His name is so often used to justify abuse.

Who would want to accept a God like this? Let alone want to hang out with Him and have a conversation? It is like getting into a relationship with a controlling abusive lover whom we worry may maim or murder us at any time. We spend all our time trying to figure out how to avoid him.

Can't we believe that we are worthy of a God who loves us *just because?* The image of a harsh, punishing God doesn't sound very godly to me. One definition of evil is the absence of God in one's life, as well as the absence of love. If love is not in the mix, then surely God is not.

Take God out of the box. You have the power to take the God that you were handed and remove Him from the box you've placed Him in. You may have been sold a bill of goods that you do not want. If the image of God you carry with you doesn't serve you, then go to the returns and exchange counter. Pick a new image and make sure it is one that inspires you. When you limit God, you limit yourself. In *Conversations with God,* Book 1, God said to Neale Donald Walsh, "Do me a favor and don't try to contain me. By the way, do yourself the same favor."

Archbishop Desmond Tutu reminds us that "God is not a Christian." Through this statement he urges us to consider how limitless God is. Allow God the respect He deserves. Take Him out of the box.

TAKE GOD OUT OF THE BOX

What ways does the image of God you currently have hurt you? Are there ways you can expand your image of God? Write a list of the characteristics of the God you want.

CHAPTER 3

Searching for God's Face

*I started searching for God's face early in life, but each crisis
pushed me further along on that quest. As I lay there, still panting
from childbirth, hearing that my long-awaited first child had died, I
asked for a hospital chaplain. A gentle Episcopal priest arrived and, at
my request and without question, performed a baptism for my daughter, despite most religious views that baptism is only for the living. His
kind act was the first step in healing my broken heart.*

*When children did enter my life through the use of the Law of
Attraction and prayer, my spiritual life was enriched. They became my
greatest teachers as to how to live in love, joy, and the present
moment. Their faces are radiant and their giggles blissful. They are
filled with God. As much as I celebrate the lessons they give me, I
continued to educate myself on the faces of God. Raising two small
babies fourteen months apart only fed my hunger for knowledge.*

*I bought a small portable tape player with earphones and listened
to spiritual tapes from many traditions as I nursed my children. I
developed my own nursing meditations that allowed me to be present in the beautiful experience of nourishing my children while connecting with the Divine.*

*By the time my third child was born, I had refined the balance of
spirituality with the realities of child rearing. My spiritual teacher
urged me to bring my baby girl to the retreats I attended. Her serene
presence helped open up some of the other attendees to the experience of merging love.*

*When my marriage was falling apart, I retreated occasionally to a
convent tucked away on an island of peace amidst the large
McMansion houses in bustling northern Virginia. I knelt in front of a
replica of the grotto in Lourdes, France, where Mary was said to have*

appeared, and asked for help from another mother as how best to take care of my children.

Even today, when I enter that garden, I feel the sense of safety I had there during troubled times. My body relaxes so much that sometimes I fall asleep in the warm sun, much to the consternation of the gentle nuns who worry about the snakes that make the garden their home.

We can widen our choices in how to find the God we want by seeing how others have found God. It is one thing to accept without question the God that has been presented to us. It is quite another to take a survey and see how limitless our choices are and how God inspires others. This exercise has helped me expand how I can see God.

I search for the many faces of God through a multitude of spiritual practices, in my extensive travels, and through the ways other people worship God. Every culture offers a different view of God. Each experience has added a new insight into the God that I now hold.

Our God-Form Manifests in Joy

Scholars talk about a "god-form" or a mental image that a person creates of a god to make sense of the great unknown. You are invited to make your own "god-form" to help you get your arms around an energy that is so big and indescribable that no one can fully define it.

Think about all the different faces of God that have been shown to you. There are the white-bearded patriarch and many Goddess images. There is the talking star in the movie *It's a Wonderful Life* and the sweet little old man George Burns played in *Oh, God.* In the book *Golfing with God* by Douglas Tatro, we are urged to see God as our golfing partner. During World War II, an American pilot said "God is my co-pilot," which later inspired a movie.

Use the Law of Attraction to help you find an image of God that you can have a conversation with—a God that YOU want. In doing so, you can use the Law of Attraction more powerfully to create a life that allows you to live at your highest potential. Perhaps you feel you already worship a God you want. But do you truly believe that this God wants to cocreate miracles in your life? Do you have that much faith in your God? Sometimes our resistance to God is imperceptible but it is there.

By creating an image of God, you attract yourself to the power of

God. There is no need to attract God into you. You don't need to pull in what is already there. You are the one holding back, not God.

Approach this assignment with lightness, playfulness, and joy, the way of a child who enters Santa's workshop. Nothing can close down a mystical connection faster than a dogged, clenched-teeth determination that "I am going to FIND God and get it right this time, by God." Both the Law of Attraction and a relationship with God work better with joy. Play at finding your God. Be like the child who picks up each toy and fiddles with it until she finds just the right one for her. God gave us joy, light, pleasure, and play so we could feel them. To be able to live our lives in a new way, we must expand and enjoy how we undertake our search for God.

Our choices in life are limitless if we can stop our limited thinking. One way to move past this is to create God in an image that reaffirms how limitless She is.

God has been portrayed in as many ways as there are people in the world. During near-death experiences, individuals report seeing the God of their faith. Christians often see Jesus or Mary. Hindus see Shiva or other deities. Buddhists see Kwan Yin, the goddess of mercy. Native Americans see animal guides.

God comes to us in a face we can recognize. There is one God— one God with many faces—bearing the faces we project on Him. Just as we are not our faces, but instead souls full of energy, so is God. There is only one power in the Universe and we are all Divine sparks of this power. God's face shows up in different ways depending on who is looking at Him. He dwells within us, around us, and in every molecule of the Universe.

Meister Johannes Eckhart, a medieval mystic, calls God a "super-essential darkness, a mystery behind mystery, a mystery within mystery that no light has penetrated." He clarifies the difference between the Godhead (the unknown Being above all nature who cannot be the object of worship) and God (the Divine power at work within the universe). He challenges us to find the face of God within ourselves.

Beneath sense perception, beneath the sensuous will, beneath the highest powers of memory, reason and reasonable will, lies the soul, the apex, the spark, the heaven within. It is here that man may find God.

—Meister Johannes Eckhart

> ## GOD'S FACE
>
> What face of God inspires you? Breathe deeply and bring
> forth this image in your mind. Check your reaction with
> your body and heart. See if there is more than one face that
> inspires you.

God and Goddess

Father, Son, and Holy Spirit are a trinity of energy. Some see God
as both male and female. The Native Americans have Mother Earth
and Father Sky, and the Hindus have Shiva and Shakti. Many religious traditions, regardless of whether they are patriarchal and insist
that God is male, have images that represent female energy. Goddess
religions came before the male images of God, and many scholars
believe that most prehistory worship was goddess centered.

All of these are archetypes of God's energy, given shape so people
can grasp God. In fact, we sometimes tease God's energy into specific
qualities so we might better understand them. I was struck by this as
I walked through Catholic churches in El Salvador and Peru filled
with multiple statues of Jesus, Mary, and saints. Each statue represented a different concern: Jesus for the Poor, Jesus for the Suffering,
Mary for the Children, Mary for Mothers. I noticed the same pattern
in China. The Buddhist temples have the laughing Buddha, the
abundant Buddha, and the Buddha of Mercy, among others. All religions have constructed archetypes to help people come to know
God.

God as the Word

The Holy Bible gives us many faces of God. A burning bush, a
dove, a star, a spark, the Christ child, and the resurrected Jesus are
just a few. In the Book of Wisdom in the Old Testament (a book
omitted from the Hebrew Bible), "Divine wisdom" is called by the
name of Sophia. Some interpret Sophia as the Holy Spirit and the
female energy of the Holy Trinity. The Book of Wisdom (7:22–26)
praises Sophia.

> *She is a breath of the power of God*
> *pure emanation of the glory of the Almighty;*
> *so nothing impure can find a way into her.*

She is a reflection of the eternal light,
untarnished mirror of God's active power,
Image of God's goodness.

This image resonates with me. Sometimes a face is not necessary, only a word. One way that religion wounded me was that the church of my upbringing prohibited women from being priests. One day I realized that, despite all the intellectual arguments, at the root of this position is the belief that women are unholy, for they are not holy enough to be priests. I asked myself why I was continuing in a faith that regards me as unholy—one that believes that I am not enough. Instead, the image of Sophia empowered me. I was so taken with envisioning Divine wisdom as female that I named my youngest daughter Sophia. My little one embodies her name.

My Search for God's Face

Looking back, I realize I have always been a seeker. I grew up attending a progressive Catholic church where, in fifth-grade Sunday school, we learned about world religions. From this, I gained respect for other traditions. There is little I remember about any other curricula in Sunday school, but I recall that year in vivid detail because it helped expand my vision.

My priest looked like Jesus with long flowing wavy hair, and when I met with the head priest as a teenager to discuss my confirmation, he told me that, although he was glad I chose to be Catholic, "there are many tickets to heaven." My parents encouraged me to visit synagogues and churches with my classmates and I was exposed to Jewish traditions, Mormon Sunday school, Episcopal rituals, Southern Baptist services, and Christian rock concerts.

When I was in elementary school, my parents drove through the Southwest to California, and, at my mother's urging, stopped at Native American reservations. I remember climbing up a ladder and then down another into the interior of a Navajo whitewashed adobe hogan, a traditional worship space.

We ventured up to a mesa rarely visited by tourists to see costumed Hopi dancers whirl around a fire. While my brothers and I watched mesmerized, a dancer dressed as a coyote paused to toss oranges to us. My mother filled our home with sculptured Kachina doll dancers, which are reputed to bring the spirit of the Gods to the Native American people.

During my years in politics, bone weary on the campaign trail from seven-day workweeks and nineteen-hour days, I felt my spirit rise as I sat in African American churches that were shaking with praise and song. I was so grateful that, when asked to speak on behalf of my candidate, I could also thank the churchgoers for reviving me.

In graduate school I traveled to Guatemala. I stood on the steps of a church in Chichicastenango to watch as statues of saints and Mary passed by, dressed in real robes, along with a statue of a tortured, bloody Jesus. The parade of religious icons meandered through the town's famous market on the backs of descendants of the Mayan Indians. When I entered the church, I was amazed to find them making offerings of Coca-Cola and rum to influence the outcome of their prayers. Their rituals combined Catholicism and ancient Indian beliefs. In a remote volcanic lake town, young children led me through back alleys to observe the worship of a rogue monk. I was asked to present an offering of cigarettes.

I visited the pyramids of the Mayans in Copán, Honduras, and felt the energetic pull of that place. I walked in the Mexican jungle and circled a small ruin dedicated to fertility rituals. I toured Incan ruins in Peru and purchased a replica of a knife I later learned was used to cut out the beating hearts of sacrificed humans (definitely not a God I want). I heard the joyful shouts in Spanish coming from Pentecostal churches in Latin America where new converts writhed in ecstasy. I even entered a voodoo shop in New Orleans, although I surely did not see God's image there.

I have been to Hindu temples where worshipers bring flowers and kiss the ground in front of statues of Shakti, Shiva, and Ghanesh. I joined them in their Sunday meal of dhal.

In rural Virginia, my children, my father, and I explored Yogaville and drank the sweet milk that is poured over Shiva's head during prayer. My children ran up a steep hill in the dark, calling back excitedly for me to join them as they went to see the large illuminated statue of Shiva.

My oldest daughter, Darya, paused in her play at the Yogaville school playground to grab my hand, telling me she had found a place for me to pray. We rounded a corner and, much to my surprise, there was a small shrine to Mary.

The Energy of the Divine Mother

My children and I visited Ammachi, called India's "hugging saint," who is said to embody the spirit of the Divine Mother and who has hugged more than thirty million people during her world-wide travels. She hugged me, blessed my family, and threw flower petals over our heads.

My children were alternatively enthralled and resistant to the experience. My eight-year-old son, Sanders, after expressing his dismay about the pending hug from Amma, found himself pressed into her large bosom for way too long while she conducted a conversation with a guru. Trying to reassure him, I started rubbing his back, causing several of the devotees to start rubbing his back, too, perhaps thinking I was sending him blessings instead of trying to keep him from freaking out—which all those additional rubbing hands did not help.

When he was free, he turned around to shoot me a piercing look of aggravation. Later, he begged me to buy him another Shiva for his altar, an image he has been drawn to since he was little.

As I waited in a long line to receive a mantra from Amma, with thousands of people wanting to get close to her, I was astounded to see my nine-year-old daughter, Darya, repeatedly walk up on the stage. She was retrieving the flowers around Amma's chair for reuse by the volunteers. We left with handfuls of flower petals, vials of Holy Water, and Sanders clutching his little Shiva.

Prayers Are a Universal Language

In Xi'an, China, I visited one of the oldest mosques in Asia and heard the call for the evening prayers in Arabic over the noise of the Mandarin Chinese being spoken in the marketplace.

I visited a Tibetan lamasery in Beijing where a huge golden Buddha filled the temple and followers spun Buddhist prayer wheels.

At the Temple of the Yellow Emperor, filled with three-thousand-year-old trees, I walked through the Gate of Heaven and climbed Prayer Stairs said to enhance the power of prayer. Worshipers lit large bundles of incense to send requests to their ancestors in heaven.

I attend Unity Church and hear our ministers, a husband and wife team, preach about our Divine perfection and the unity of all of us. One summer each Sunday was devoted to a major religion from Taoism to Islam, an adult experience reminiscent of my positive childhood Sunday school.

I still find some nourishment from the occasional Catholic Mass and receive direction from progressive clergy, yet find that my spiritual diet needs additional food. I consider myself a cultural Catholic, one who honors the spiritual traditions of my ancestors.

Four times a year, I drive to a healing center in Maryland to sit in a Native American sweat lodge to sweat out and let go of all that doesn't serve me. In that sacred circle, with the large glowing rocks hissing steam amid the smell of burning sweet grass, I talk with other women about Mother Earth, Father Sky, and the Great Mystery.

I was moved and inspired when I read Marianne Williamson's *Return to Love*, which is based on *A Course in Miracles*. The primary message is one of forgiveness and love, and I slowly explore the richness of this teaching.

Some of my deepest experiences have occurred in Diamond Approach spiritual retreat workshops, something I have participated in since 1994. In this new teaching, a mixture of Western psychology, Eastern meditation, Gurdjieff theory, and Sufi concepts, founded by A. H. Almaas, we rarely speak directly of God, yet God is infused in the work.

It is there, working one-on-one with my spiritual teacher, Deane Shank, that I often experience the most intense feelings of God. I feel my soul blossoming like a rosebud opening to the sun. I watch friends, who have attended with me over the years, soften and relax into their inner beauty.

Recognizing That God Is Everywhere

I see God as I watch the weathered faces of the Tibetan lamas who have found refuge in my hometown of Charlottesville, Virginia. I hear them chant their repetitive prayers and I listen to their teachings.

I see the face of God when I sit atop a mountain in Virginia's Blue Ridge, level to the clouds, looking down at the vastness of the valley.

I see God when I climb the Great Wall of China and am moved to tears over the abundance and beauty of my life.

I see God as I look at the ocean waves, powerfully crashing, and returning again and again.

I see God as I sit writing on the porch of a remote mountain cabin as the dancing water of two streams meet.

I see God in the sunset, in the dew drop, in the whir of a dragonfly's wing, and in the curve of a child's finger.

God has a different face to everyone. For me, to see how limitless our choices are helps me choose images that speak directly to me.

I know I don't have to find God in all these places. I know God is right here, right now. I know God is all around me and inside me. Yet to know I can pick an image from such an abundant buffet helps me connect more intensely. I am able to identify many faces of the God I want.

Create, Don't Limit

People throughout the world have created images to represent the unknowable, the indescribable, the Great Mystery. I urge you to create your own image, with this caveat: **Do not be bound by it.** Giving God a face is a way to allow us to relate to God. But do not recreate the same trap you fell into when you accepted someone else's image. Remember, God is bigger than any face you give Him.

This is why God warned the Israelites against creating graven idols. This is why the Muslims have no image of Allah. It is another way to put God in a box. When we take a multidimensional God and make Him one-dimensional, we limit God and ourselves.

Find God in the forms that inspire you. God is God. We are not required to see God in the way tradition has taught us. We can manifest our own relationship with God. We may not want the God of traditional religions or a patriarchal society. We may not want an Old Testament or New Testament God. We need to envision a friendship with God in which we have a comfortable conversation.

NO HOLDS BARRED

What holds you back from accepting the God you want? Write at least ten answers to this question—whatever first comes into your mind. Now flip the question. What allows you to accept the God you want?

Growing into an Adult Relationship with God

Now that you have started to find the God you want, the challenge is whether you can accept Her. As a coach who helps people reach their goals, I know that we often resist what we say we want most. Something causes us to hold back or even to self-sabotage.

If we can look at, and deal with, what holds us back, often we can move forward.

You have an opportunity to step into a more powerful place of being and relating. Even if you had only healthy messages about God, part of growing into a spiritual relationship is moving into a bigger version of God. If God is wide and vast and unknowable, then God can fill all the faces and all the spaces you can give Him.

When I listen quietly to God, this is what I hear:

If you view me with love, if you come from a place of love,
you cannot go wrong, no matter what face you put on me.

When I was a child, I talked like a child, I thought like a
child, I reasoned like a child. When I became an adult, I
put away childish things.

—1 Corinthians 13:11

Don't stay in a child's role, accepting everything you have been told and seeing a smaller God. Put away that childish, passive way of being. Move into having a proactive adult relationship with God. Just as our relationship with our parents changes as we become adults, so does our relationship with God. As adults we realize that our parents are more complex and multidimensional than we believed as children. We can see more clearly through our adult eyes. So it is with God.

Mystics throughout history have trouble finding the words that can contain the fullness of God. Angela of Foligno wrote in *The Book of Divine Consolation* in the fifteenth century: "And when I looked, I beheld God who spake with me. But if thou seekest to know that which I beheld, I can tell thee nothing, save that I beheld a fulness and a clearness, and felt them within me so abundantly that I can in no wise describe it, nor give any likeness thereof."

This is the paradox. Find a face that you can relate to, an image you can have a conversation with, a name that you can call. Yet always know that whatever you have created, God is so much more.

CHAPTER 4

Feeling God

I sat in disbelief in an orange jumpsuit at 3:00 a.m. on a cold cement bench in the women's holding cell of the Fairfax County Jail. I was in the cell with eight other women, some drunk, others crying, and one talking tough to establish her alpha status. My mind was trying to grasp my predicament.

I was a successful corporate coach who worked with government officials—including police chiefs and officers—and a highly educated suburban mother who drove a mini-van and tried to live a life guided by spiritual values. One of my girlfriends was the sheriff in a neighboring community. But, here I was, sitting in jail, booked as a criminal.

On my way home from a spiritual gathering, I had been pulled over by four police cars, officers approaching my van from both sides. This was clearly not a standard traffic stop for having tags that had expired twelve days before. In front of my young children, I was taken out of my van, patted down, handcuffed with my hands behind my back, and put in the back of a police cruiser. I was in shock.

I sat with my head in my arms and prayed that I would feel God's presence as strongly in that cold cell as I had a few hours before in a room filled with worshipers chanting about God's greatness.

I asked for God's help and guidance and it came. By 7:00 a.m., my friend Ann had bailed me out and I was reunited with my children.

As I sat in the jail cell after being arrested, I knew that I had created this crisis by my feelings. I was being handed one mega lesson about the Law of Attraction. I wasn't sure at first what I had done to pull in the problem but I knew I needed help to reverse a disaster of cosmic proportions. What I needed was Divine intervention. I really needed to *feel* God's presence.

God's hand softened the blow for me that night. I felt God with me. Although my thoughts and feelings had created the crisis, once I asked for help, God's presence guided my thoughts and feelings. God filled my heart with a gentle knowing and a warm, calm heat. Slowly I was delivered from my dilemma.

I know this from the kindness of the arresting woman officer who gently took me to the magistrate who looked at me, said "I believe you," and gave me a lower bond.

I know this from the direction I received about my choices. As I stood by the telephone, looking at flyers advertising bail bondsmen and praying for guidance, I felt pulled to call one bail bondsman over all the others, only to find out later that despite other ads claiming night availability, he was the only one who really did work nights.

Later, I discovered that if he and my friend had failed to start the process to bail me out before six that morning, I would have spent the whole next day and another night in jail.

Sitting on the hard cement bench praying for help, I am sure God helped keep me safe from an aggressive female who was berating the other women.

The greatest blessing was to have my dear friend Ann traveling with me. Afterward I realized that, if she had not been there, my children would have been placed in temporary foster care. The thought they could have been taken from me is too horrifying for me to consider, even now.

Pulling in One Mega Problem

I knew I had created this mega problem. But I needed guidance on what I had done to attract jail time! The irony was that I had felt so peaceful and inspired before this happened. We were traveling back from a day spent with the guru Ammachi, the Indian "hugging saint." She had blessed and given mantras to Ann and me. How did I create this reality after such an experience? What kind of cosmic joke was this for a woman who regularly coached police chiefs?

I discovered later that my arrest was because of a twenty-dollar bounced check caused by money stolen from my checking account—which I had paid back six months earlier. Because of a clerical error, I had been listed as not paying and in contempt of court, a fact that had never been served to me because, for some unknown reason, they had me classified as a fugitive from justice.

Unbeknownst to me, I had been considered a fugitive for six months—the same period that I had repeatedly walked into police departments to coach. The officers would have been required to arrest me if they had known about it.

An Improbable Confluence of Events

One of the police chiefs I worked for said, in reviewing my situation, that it was the most unusual and improbable confluence of events he had ever seen. His words confirmed to me that I had indeed attracted this situation into my life and somewhere there was a reason for it. I wanted to learn this reason, this lesson, so I would never create it again.

I struggled to understand. Eventually, I realized that my problem lay deep within my feelings, that it wasn't about what I was thinking or feeling *that* day, but from the overall energy that I carried with me *each* day. It was because there were challenges I needed to move through in my life before I was able to truly RECEIVE all that I wanted.

That same month I was negotiating a book contract to write about the Law of Attraction. I had used the Law of Attraction to create this opportunity: I asked for it, I felt it coming, and it came. I held a vision that I would write a book and a publisher fell into my lap.

I was moving into my power—and underneath all the optimism and visioning, underneath all the work I had done to increase my confidence and self-esteem—was a feeling that I had better not get too big for my britches. There were many reasons for this, but the bottom line was I still did not love myself enough to receive all the grandness life has to offer me.

Yes, there were some basic issues I needed to pay attention to, details such as a checkbook transactions and car tags, and by not paying attention, I had unconsciously been self-sabotaging and unloving to myself. But also deep inside me, there were places in which I was holding myself back, mostly out of fear. I truly believed that it was dangerous to get too big, too powerful, and too successful.

Healing through Feeling

If you drill down into the beliefs you have held since childhood, do you have the same trepidation? Do you still have an issue that isn't fully healed, no matter how many affirmations you do or how much self-discovery you engage in?

Receiving what we want to attract into our life is where most of us falter because, deep down, we don't believe we are worthy enough. Or that it will really come. Or that we are that powerful. Or that God loves us that much.

As we invite God into our heart, we can heal. We begin to acutely feel Her presence residing in us. Soon we call to God without a crisis that demands the call.

Much more important than how we see God is allowing ourselves to feel God. God makes His presence known all the time. Yet we often doubt our own experiences, believing we made them up.

Our image of a miracle is that it announces itself with lots of smoke and thunder. But if we are truthful to ourselves, we can tell when we have had Divine intervention in our life by how we *feel*. While I was in jail, I didn't start feeling calm because I knew I was going to get out. In fact, I was unable to reach anyone and had no idea I was going to be released until the guard called me out. My calmness came from a presence that descended on me. Nothing had changed, really. I know a miracle occurred because of how I *felt*. I could feel the presence of God manifested in my calmness and the warmth in my heart. Someone had reminded me that I was not alone.

Carl Jung used to have a sign over his doorway that read: *"Called or uncalled, God is present."*

Let us have that sign posted over the doorway to our hearts to remind us that God is present. All we have to do is wake up to that reality. When we listen to our feelings, without rationalizing in our minds, we can feel God is present. Then we become courageous enough to call for God.

Feelings Are the Pathway to God

Our feelings are our direct pathway to God. When people try to find God through the mind, they end up frustrated.

Spiritual teacher and medical intuitive Caroline Myss has stories of workshop participants who tried to find God through dedicated study, only to feel like failures. Her advice to each of them was to stop searching with the mind and open the heart.

While I was working on this chapter, I felt moved to pull a card from the *Conversations with God ReMINDer* deck. Although I often receive stunning guidance from card decks, I continue to be in awe of the messages I get. The quote I pulled was: *"Feeling is the language of the soul."*

Feeling *IS* the language of the soul. When we really feel our feelings, we see the truth in our lives. Our souls are always pushing us toward the truth while our minds are trying to shield us from it. God wants us to live lives of love and truth. When we are out of alignment, our feelings arise to tell us so.

Feelings Are God's Pathway to Us

In Western culture, we are taught to discount our feelings. We worship rational thought. Rational thought ensures we won't have to make major changes, we don't have to feel uncomfortable about our lives, and we won't have to access a realm that is unknowable. Feelings challenge all this. Feelings are seen as too messy, too unpredictable, and uncontrollable. They become this way the more we suppress them, until they burst out like a dam breaking. Many nervous breakdowns are caused by stuffing feelings until they can't be held in anymore. What a gift when all those feelings rush out. They are opportunities for us to hear God without our minds getting in the way. In the mystical tradition, breakdowns have been related to individuals opening up to Divine union, "spiritual nervous breakdowns," according to Myss. For many, it is the first time they are intensely *feeling* their feelings.

I know from experience. When I was twenty-nine years old, all the feelings that I had been pushing down came roaring out. I had just gotten married eighteen months before and, within two weeks of my marriage, my husband had flipped from adoring me to despising me. I had been on a pedestal and then felt like I was thrown on the garbage heap. I could do nothing right, no matter how hard I tried. It was a familiar pattern I had experienced since childhood.

I went into a reaction of what I now call "defiant denial" about the toxicity of my marriage. No one was going to know how bad it was—including me. I became a master at presenting the image of a happy marriage, while desperately dragging my husband to marriage counselors so we could get "fixed." I learned early in life that love and pain go together. Because that is what I had known, I had recreated it.

I had many messages from God trying to guide me out of this mess, ranging from feelings to perceptive observations from friends, but I was unwilling to hear them. I wanted to be in denial, and if I heard that guidance, it would mean I would have to make a change and leave my husband. Tragically, I was more frightened of being alone than I was of being with someone who mistreated me.

Someone's Knocking on Your Door

What pushed me over the edge was that my work environment started to replicate my home life. I had risen quickly in politics and, six months into my marriage, had been appointed Deputy Director of Communications for a new governor. It turned out to be a toxic environment as well. I sat at my desk every day and watched the winds shift as to who was on top and who was on bottom.

I was able to keep my head down and not be a direct target, but my career reached a crisis when I was asked to lie to the media about a state police investigation. I faced a moral dilemma and a professional one: To lie would be against my integrity, could subject me to a grand jury investigation, and could ruin my credibility with the media forever.

I shut down emotionally. I drove the entire way home in the dark on the interstate without remembering to turn my headlights on, an apt metaphor for how I was living my life. I had been pushing down all my feelings of grief, anger, and despair into my belly and it ached with pain. My body finally fell apart from the effort. I could not get out of bed for a week. I was diagnosed with irritable bowel syndrome, as my body tried to rid itself of all that toxic buildup. Friends would take me to lunch and I felt like I was staring at them numbly through a plate-glass window. I wanted to knock out the window between us to reach them but felt paralyzed.

At that time, I only had the strength and perspective to deal with the fallout from my job, not my marriage. My husband and I made a radical decision and quit our jobs to go to graduate school. It was my first lesson in the rewards of taking a risk. I loved the intellectual stimulation and freedom academia offered. In graduate school, I was exposed to people who were doing Diamond Approach spiritual work, a practice that has revolutionized my life and opened my heart. And my body regained some equilibrium.

I believe that God was knocking on the door of my feelings, a door that I had barricaded. When I refused to answer, She reached me through my body. As with other major decisions in my life, I had to fall apart in order to start anew. I don't seem to be able to make transitions without a crisis. At twenty-nine, I was only able to take a baby step toward a life of love and truth, but that step started me on a more deliberate spiritual path.

Crisis Conversations

There is nothing like a crisis to make us search for God. We may spend most of our life holding God at bay, but when we are in deep doo-doo, we want to know where the hell (or Heaven) He is! We want Him now, *right now*, even if we never wanted Him before.

Sometimes I picture us as angry teenagers who don't want our parents around, except when we really need them to rescue us from whatever jam we create. Just like teenagers, we are resistant to appearing in public with our parents and we don't want to give them much credit— but when we are in trouble, we turn to them because we know they love us. As teenagers, we depend more on our parents than we admit even to ourselves. Many of us act the same way with God.

A crisis provides an opportunity to reach out for God. We are forced to move temporarily past our blocks. Our fear or grief pushes past our resistance to call out to God for help. The fear of the moment takes us right into our feelings. And for a brief time, our heads get out of the way.

For many of us, it is the only time we have a conversation with God. Crisis can be the one time when we are willing to consider asking God into our lives. We pray fervently, desperately, for some relief. We beg for a specific outcome. Sometimes our faces are tear-streaked from pain and other times our bodies are stiff with alarm.

We may be angry at ourselves for thinking God can help us, but we ask anyway. Sometimes we allow ourselves to reach out only because it's on behalf of our loved ones and not ourselves. We often apologize, explain, or rationalize to God why it has taken us so long to establish contact.

We do it awkwardly, feeling self-conscious and unschooled, but we do it. Our intense feelings in that moment mow over our sense of inadequacy so that we make the connection we have resisted in the past. And we are shocked when we get an answer. For many of us, a crisis conversation ends up changing our lives and our relationship with God.

The world is filled with stories of people who did not know how to pray but learned in crisis. Some atheists admit to praying when they are in danger. Many a person has had a spiritual transformation at a twelve-step meeting after hitting rock bottom.

Reverend Stretton Smith speaks eloquently about entering his first Alcoholics Anonymous meeting as a spiritual cynic, one who had denied the existence of God his entire life and enjoyed devastating others' spirituality. During the meeting, no one mentioned the word "God" or the word "love." Yet by the time Stretton got out of his chair at the end of the meeting, he reports that he intuitively knew that God existed. Smith went on to become a nationally recognized Unity minister who developed the 4T Prosperity Program. His writings have inspired thousands of people about the power of inviting God into every aspect of their lives and creating the life they want through thought, feeling, and prayer.

Amazing Grace

A famous crisis conversation ended up birthing the beloved hymn "Amazing Grace," which sums up the experience of receiving God's grace. The author, John Newton, first went to sea when he was eleven years old, with his father, the commander of a merchant ship. After his father retired, Newton was pressed into service on a man-of-war where he found the conditions dismal. He deserted, but was soon recaptured, publicly flogged, and demoted. At his own request, he was exchanged into service on a slave ship. There he became the servant of a slave trader and was brutally abused. A sea captain who had known Newton's father rescued him, and Newton eventually went on to become captain of a slave ship.

Newton's mother, who died while he was a child, had given him some early religious instruction, but as an adult, he offered no religious convictions. On May 10, 1748, during a violent storm, he experienced what he would refer to later as his "great deliverance." His journal reveals that he believed the ship was going to sink and he exclaimed, "Lord, have mercy upon us."

Later, in his cabin, he reflected on what he had said and began to believe that God had addressed him through the storm and that grace had begun to work for him in an amazing way.

He became a Christian, though he continued in slave trading. Years later, he left the slave trade, and eventually became a minister and a spokesman against slavery.

Newton describes his crisis conversation in his song:

> *How precious did that Grace appear,*
> *the hour I first believed.*
> *Through many dangers,*
> *toils and snares,*
> *we have already come.*
> *'Twas Grace that brought us safe thus far,*

and Grace will lead us home.
The Lord has promised good to me,
His word my hope secures.

"Amazing Grace" is considered one of the top forty-five Christian hymns in the world. The lyrics *"Amazing Grace, how sweet the sound, that saved a wretch like me. I once was lost but now am found, was blind, but now, I see"* have not only touched churchgoers but are a favorite with supporters of freedom and human rights, both Christian and non-Christian.

"Amazing Grace" was sung during civil rights marches, anti-apartheid protests, and peace rallies. While walking the Trail of Tears, the Cherokee were not always able to give their dead a full burial. Instead, the singing of "Amazing Grace" had to suffice. "Amazing Grace" is often considered the Cherokee National Anthem.

John Newton's crisis conversation with God ended up inspiring untold numbers of people struggling in their own lives and those dedicated to improving many lives through social justice.

A Voice in the Dark

Elizabeth Gilbert writes with wit and passion in *Eat, Pray, Love* about her crisis conversation with God while she was deciding whether to leave her marriage. Every night she wept into the wee hours despairing about what to do. One night, she begged God for guidance. God answered her in the best way possible for someone distraught in the middle of the night: God told her to go back to bed. Gilbert writes that she knew it was God because she could feel God. Her sobbing stopped suddenly and she felt calm. This initial conversation sent her on a journey around the world to feel a deeper connection with her God.

My Crisis Conversation

My most dramatic crisis conversation with God occurred in the hospital after I had surgery to repair damage done by childbirth. I had begun to realize that my thirteen-year marriage was toxic and that, for me to survive and thrive, I needed to leave it. I had given my husband a year to change. We were approaching the deadline and, although initially there had been improvement, it was clear he was unable to change. He wanted to change, he really did, and in fact he was suffering, too. He was just not capable of it. Stress triggered him into cycles of depression and aggression. I contributed to it by being anxious, controlling, and co-dependent. Things went from bad to worse when he was fired from his job and I had to move my surgery up before we lost his insurance. The anticipation of taking care of three small children for at least six weeks while his wife recovered from surgery triggered his abusive behavior.

Two days before I went into the hospital, my husband looked me squarely in the eye and said, "I hope you die on the operating table." I felt as if a knife had been plunged into my stomach. I walked around stunned for two days, with fear spiraling out of control.

I had been verbally abused and sometimes physically abused since our first year of marriage. It was the classic abuse pattern that kept me sucked in because just when it got bad enough, he would turn into the adoring husband I first married and we would have a honeymoon period. I believed that because I was not being beaten—just shoved, kicked, or having things thrown at me—that I was not being abused. He seemed to disassociate when he had done something terrible, as if his mind would not accept that he could have done it. His moods would cycle from playful happiness to suicidal despair and depression, and then turn into intense rages. Many times, I had run outside in a nightgown and bare feet in the snow to hide from him, sometimes with a baby at my breast. During his rages, he would tell me in detail how he would murder me, but I somehow rationalized these threats away.

This time though, with surgery looming, my survival felt threatened. Trying to get reassurance, I went back to him a day later and asked if he meant it. His answer was that if he could, he would "pull the plug."

The morning of the surgery, I was a wreck. When my mom arrived to take care of our children, I pulled her aside and told her I was giving her medical authority to make decisions for me and removing this authority from my husband.

Just as I had during much of my marriage, I kept trying to push down how hurt and fearful I felt while I waited in pre-op. Although my heart was pounding and my stomach churning, my mind was busy rationalizing why the man I loved would have said something so devastating to me. But then my mind had to get out of the way when I was put under anesthesia. As I came out of unconsciousness, my heart came up in full force, unblocked by my rationalizing mind. I woke up screaming and crying and telling the doctors and nurses that my husband had wanted me to die and, thank God, I hadn't.

When he caught up to my gurney as it was being pushed from surgery, I turned my face away from him and asked a nurse to keep him out of my room. It was like a door had closed in my heart while I was under anesthesia, and when I awoke, I was no longer in love with him or under his power.

That night, in deep physical and emotional pain, attached to a morphine drip, I tossed and turned, unable to sleep. Every time I dozed off, I saw a large hand with a TV remote turn on the scene when my husband told me he wanted me to die. The hand would then rewind the scene and play it again. I had to watch that scene over and over again until I woke sobbing.

I finally cried out, "God, why are you doing this to me?" And I heard an answer. A gentle, loving, firm answer: "So you will finally GET it, Michelle."

The next morning, I told my husband I wanted a divorce. I never spent another night in the same house with him. I started out my life as a single mom of three young children weak from surgery and in six weeks of intensive recovery, but I was free from a toxic life.

It took two protective orders and a no-contact order before HE got it and let me go. He has grown from this experience and now we coparent our children with increasing cooperation and respect, but it was a rocky start. I understand much more now about what caused him to act the way he did and what I did to contribute to it, and I have forgiven him, but I will not allow myself ever to be treated like that again. I had given him *my* power.

I see the young woman I was with compassion because she was doing the best she could, but now I know better. Most important, I realize that I was engaging in a form of self-hatred to have lived with vicious verbal and physical abuse as long as I did.

CRISIS CONVERSATION

Think back to a crisis conversation you had with God, even if it was a fleeting moment of "Please, God, don't let this car hit me." How did you feel during the experience?

God Awakens Us

This was the first time I had a two-way conversation with God— when I got an answer right back. I had been in such denial and co-dependence in my marriage for so long that God had to be really clear with me. It felt like I was seeing a deprogramming tape used for someone who had been brainwashed!

Now I tell people that when I came out of anesthesia, I truly woke up for the first time in my life. I had been asleep to the reality of my life. When I woke up, I realized I had been living a nightmare. My father sent me an encouraging email titled "sleeping beauty has awakened."

Sometimes our crises are necessary. We get a strong whack on the head to try to get us to pay attention to the choices we have. A crisis conversation is a gift God gives us to wake up to our lives.

LIVING IN YOUR TRUTH

Breathe into your body. How do you feel right now? Are you living in your truth?

Have there been times when you have not lived in your truth?

When you were in crisis, did your feelings alert you that you were living out of your truth?

Remember, God Is Self-Love

God is love and our Divine nature is love. Learning to love ourselves and others is our life's work. When we live our lives in a way in which we do not love ourselves or others, a crisis often erupts to wake us up. We create it on a subconscious level sometimes, to force ourselves to change. Reverend Stretton Smith was not living in love by being an alcoholic. John Newton was not living in love by engaging in the slave trade. Elizabeth Gilbert was not living in love by staying where she felt trapped and hopeless. And I was not living in love by staying in a painful marriage.

It took me years to realize that being "in love" with someone who abused me was a form of self-hatred. I had linked love with pain; I did not truly know what love was like. Many of us have distorted versions of what we think love is. Remember, real love always allows us to be the highest, best version of ourselves. It lifts us up instead of dragging us down. If we want to use the Law of Love, also known as the Law of Attraction, we need to really feel love. This means being able to feel self-love. Self-love is remembering our power no matter what is happening to us.

> ## HAVE YOU LIVED IN LOVE?
> List the ways you have not lived in love for yourself. How did you know? List the ways you have lived in love. How did you know?

Bargaining with God

Crisis conversations can lead us to God, but sometimes we operate out of an old mind-set of who God is. Often we bargain like children: "If you do this, I'll do this." These bargains can set us up for more pain. We keep them even if they are not the right course of action or we break them and then feel guilty.

We do not need to bargain with God! Having a relationship with God is not like going to a flea market and bargaining on a price. It is not like begging Daddy for his car keys, or writing a letter to Santa Claus saying you will be good girl if you get the newest model of Barbie. It is not like being in a dysfunctional partnership in which the only way you are going to get something you want is to give up something else.

Bargaining is based on the belief that God's love for us is conditional, that if we do something for God—or stop doing something—God will do something for us. The Old Testament did portray a bargaining God, but Jesus' message in the New Testament was about forgiveness and unconditional love from God.

Unconditional love means that love rains down on us all the time. The flowers don't have to ask for the rain and the sun. It is provided for them. We are like God's flowers. We merely have to turn our faces toward God like flowers do toward the sun.

> ## BARGAIN-FREE ZONE
> Breathe deeply and relax. Feel into your heart. Tell your mind to hush. Ask God for something. Give yourself permission to just ask, and do not promise anything in return.

Faith Based on Feelings

Mystics seek direct contact with God. Unlike theologians who deal in rational thought, mystics ground themselves in feeling. They focus on the mystery rather than the explanation. Mystics understand that the unknown cannot be known. They do not try to box God in because they know that God is indescribable.

> The thinkers of Classical Antiquity and the fathers of the Church had elevated man's rationality, his ability to reason logically and without the subjectivity of emotions, to a divine gift which marked the road to salvation. . . .
>
> [The counterpoint to this was mysticism which] asserted that transcendent knowledge came not as a product of rational thought, but as a result of a way of life, of individual inspiration and sudden revelatory insight.

—Gerda Lerner, *The Creation of Feminist Consciousness*, pages 65 and 66

Alan Watts, an Eastern philosopher and former Episcopal priest, argued in his lectures that there are those who base their faith in God on text, and those who base it on mystical experience. Those who are text-based feel the need to defend their position quite rigidly because if one plank is pulled out, the whole foundation falls in, whether the text is the Bible, the Koran, or the Bhagavad Gita. Those who have a mystical connection know from their own experience that God is there. If challenged, they merely remember their life-changing experiences.

I read recently in the *Washington Post* about a biblical scholar who had been a devout fundamentalist Christian. He had devoted his life to studying the Bible because it was on this text that he had based his faith. When he discovered there were some details in the Bible that did not add up to historical fact, his religious faith fell apart. He became angry and switched to proving that Christianity was based on deception. I remember reading the article and thinking about how black and white he was in his faith. Because each fact did not line up exactly right, his whole belief system was destroyed. This comes from knowing God intellectually, in one's mind only, not deeply in one's heart.

Faith means to take a leap, despite gaps in logic. If you have connected with God through your feelings, you KNOW God is.

The Church of Logic

When we base our relationship with God on feelings, we have a direct experience. Yet our head is always going to tell us to discount our mystical experience. It will tell us we are not really having it.

We can have a burning bush or a voice booming at us, and we will find a way to explain it away. There have been many signs from God, from the Red Sea opening and manna from heaven to Jesus walking on water and rising from the dead. And yet so many of us doubt. The more dramatic the sign, the more doubt people have about it.

God usually speaks to us much more subtly. Elijah from the Old Testament faced earthquakes and thunder, only to discover God in a small, quiet voice.

In Western culture, we worship logical thought—the Church of Logic. In doing so, we devalue feelings and intuition, yet how many times have our heads led us astray? When our guts tell us that a person cannot be trusted, or that we really should drive a different way home, we often second-guess ourselves because we think we are not being logical. Our heads get in the way of true wisdom because our feelings are not valued.

When we don't value our feelings or don't honor what our body is telling us, we are ignoring the ways that God is talking to us. Sometime we have to relearn how to trust God's voice.

At spiritual retreats, people often ask shyly about an experience they had, as if they need confirmation that it is God. If the leader validates it, they visibly relax and trust the experience. If, for some reason, their experience is not acknowledged, then they devalue the experience.

A. H. Almaas, the founder of the Diamond Approach Work, was working with a Gurdjieff teacher early in his spiritual development. He kept seeing colors and would go and talk to the master about it. The master kept dismissing it because it wasn't what he believed Almaas was supposed to see at the time nor what the teacher considered an important experience. Almaas trusted himself and his spiritual unfolding and went on to found a spiritual practice based on his experiences.

Cut Off Your Head

Our feelings are our pathway to God and the way that God most often connects with us. Our heads can steamroll over the still, quiet voice. The Buddhist tradition has a saying that one must cut off one's head to know God. Buddhist monks, both men and women, cut off all their hair to be symbolically closer to God. Get out of your own way. Get your head out of the way. Feel God. Really feel God.

Rumi, the great Sufi mystic poet, wrote: "If knowledge of mysteries comes after emptiness of mind, that is Illumination of heart." There is another Buddhist saying: if you see the Buddha on the road, kill him. This means that if you think you can truly recognize the Buddha and fully understand all the mystery, then you need to rid yourself of this delusion. Whether you metaphorically cut your head off, kill the Buddha, or merely empty your mind as Rumi guides, true knowledge and guidance reside in the heart and body.

Sense the fullness and richness that reside in your heart space. Allow the wisdom of your body to arise and move your head out of the way. If something feels right, on some deep level that calls out to your soul, then do it. If something feels wrong, this is a warning to heed.

The Titanic of Doubt

The *Titanic* was considered an unsinkable ship. Each decision that brought it closer to disaster, from having too few lifeboats to ramming into an iceberg to other ships ignoring the SOS from an unsinkable ship, was based on logic. Yet something was terribly wrong. The fact that some were still arguing the point while it was sinking is evidence that our minds often inhibit our deeper wisdom.

The Many Feelings of God Are Like the Many Faces of God

Our emotions are a Geiger counter picking up the vibration of God like a Geiger counter picks up the invisible presence of radiation. We feel God in our lives all the time, but we may not recognize it. Every time we feel love, we feel God. Every time we feel joy, gratitude, appreciation, compassion, or empathy, we feel God.

When we can feel into our hearts, we remember that God is right next to us. It is like calling out for Mother in the middle of the night, only to open your eyes and find out she is holding you. It is like looking for something, only to realize it is in front of you.

God can feel like a friend. She can feel like a loving parent to guide, protect, and nurture us. Rumi's poetry portrays God as the Beloved, a lover who so satisfies our every desire that we are drunk with love for Her.

There is nothing broader, wider, or deeper than God's love. Love is like the endless ocean with nothing containing it. God is more than seeing a face and hearing a voice. God is feeling. Embrace this feeling and you embrace yourself.

CHAPTER 5

Your Invisible Companion

I was meditating at a spiritual retreat when suddenly I heard a loud rushing sound, like a powerful river, passing by my right side. Stunned, I struggled to get my mind around this feeling that a river was rushing right past me as I sat in a quiet room. I sensed it was a river of energy that carried along my life and I was being told to start going with the current.

Sometimes God appears in your life in a form different from what you expected. There are times when God's hand is at work in your life in ways that you reject at the time, only to see the wisdom later. Be alert and look for where God appears. You can play at it like the game Hitchcock movie fans enjoy in which they look for Alfred Hitchcock hidden in plain view in all of his movies. God, too, is hidden in plain view.

See the Miracle

I have heard the crying of your heart. I have seen the searching of your soul. I know how deeply you have desired the Truth. In pain have you called out for it, and in joy. Unendingly you have beseeched Me. Show Myself. Explain Myself. Reveal Myself.

—Neale Donald Walsch, *Conversations with God, Book 1*, page 58

We demand that God show Himself and yet we don't expect Him to do so. Miracles can happen right in front of our eyes and we may still not expect God's presence. When Jesus healed people in front of crowds of onlookers, there were always doubters. Thomas had to put his hand into the wound in Jesus' side to verify it was truly Jesus. Being able to expect God to BE HERE NOW is a stretch for some. God seems so far away. They may have prayed for something that did not come. Many a child has been heartbroken when they prayed for a bicycle that did not appear or for something serious, like healing an ill family member who eventually died.

My son has asked me many times why God let his parents get divorced, despite his prayers. For me the answer is clear: God saw two people suffering deeply and released us. Small children cannot see that. They know only the pain they feel.

I will never forget the grief on my son's face when we all watched *The Secret* DVD and he turned to me and said, "I did not attract my parents' divorce."

I assured him that he did not. Sometimes we cannot know why something happened, even if there is a good reason. My son, with his father's gift of analytical analysis and high IQ coupled with my intuition and emotional intelligence, is special because of the two parents he had, regardless of whether they could stay together.

The Angel on Your Shoulder

Sometimes things do not work out the way we want because God is protecting us.

One of my dearest friends was moved to help when the tsunami hit Indonesia. She organized a fundraiser and in a short amount of time people banded together to help her put on a high-profile event that was covered on the TV news. She felt frustrated though that the charity she wanted to donate the money to was so concerned about the way the money was being handled.

Although I tried to assure her it was because money is often collected and not turned in or someone involved is not ethical, she was experiencing the concerns as doubt about her personal integrity. She instituted all the safeguards the charity asked for but she no longer felt the same joy or appreciation for how powerful her event was.

Almost four months later, I discovered that one of the chief people she was working with had been fired for embezzlement and that this was a pattern for this individual. When I told my friend, her reaction was that God had been protecting her and the event. She said, "Oh, my God, I had an angel watching over me and I didn't know it. That money made it to the right place and all I could see was the obstacles."

Sometimes it makes no sense to us why something happens but later we see the Divine wisdom in it.

Expect God's Compassion

Sometimes, although we will never understand a loss, when we look back on the landscape of our lives, we would not change what came out of it. God is there with us throughout it all, even when we do not understand the "why." If you look for God's presence, He is always there. Not only can you expect it, you can count on it.

You will grieve but your grief will turn to joy. A woman giving birth to a child has pain because her time has come; but when her baby is born she forgets the anguish because of her joy that a child is born into the world. So with you.

—John 16:20–22

Even in crisis there is always something to learn, and in tragedy there is always a gift.

My most dramatic example of this was the death of my first child, Lilia Epiphany. After years of infertility and thousands of dollars of fertility treatments, I became pregnant with a baby girl through invasive surgery. Five months into the pregnancy, she was diagnosed in utero with a severe heart defect.

This happened back in the days when I thought through sheer willpower and force I could create the outcomes I wanted. After the initial shock, I went into overdrive to save her even when the ultrasound showed she had only the left ventricle of her heart. I did research on pediatric heart surgery, joined parent support groups, and interviewed doctors, hospitals, and labor coaches.

I ended up choosing Duke Medical Center because it had a world-class pediatric heart surgeon. Because of this choice, I had to live by myself, four hours away from my home and husband, during my last month of pregnancy. Each week, except for a week-long stay with my brother, I lived in the home of strangers kind enough to take me in.

I did all this to save my baby. God had brought her to me against all odds. I knew He would not take her from me. So when she died, I stumbled around in disbelief. The first night back in my home, I woke up with the searing sensation of a knife being plunged through my heart.

Words cannot begin to describe the depth of pain and grief I carried. Studies indicate that the most painful death to recover from is the death of a child. I can attest to the validity of this. For months, my eyes were vacant and my heart so broken that I could barely get through the day. During this time, I wrote a poem about my heart resembling the broken pieces of a fragile teacup that I was trying to glue back together. I felt broken like bone china shattered into a thousand little slivers of glass.

I will never know the "why" and looking for it is a waste of time. What I do know is that it marked a time of spiritual transformation for me. I deepened my connection with God. I learned to surrender my life. I realized I could not create my life through sheer force of will and that I needed to give up control to God, while learning to cocreate with God to manifest the life I wanted. I started to expect God to show up and accepted that She would.

A little more than a year later, I was blessed with the pregnancy of my little boy, Sanders, and a few months later, I adopted my little girl, Darya. It was unlikely I would have gotten pregnant with Sanders so soon if I had been coping with the severe heart problems of my first child. And I know I would not have traveled to Russia to get my baby girl, Darya. It is so clear that these two children were meant to be in my life. I hesitate to say that Lilia died so that Darya and Sanders would come to me, but I feel blessed every day they are with me.

Lilia's death marked the birth of my new life.

Expect That God Is with You

Anyone who has been through a crisis knows it can provoke a crisis of faith. Not only do we stop expecting God to be with us, but we wonder if God even cares.

When my stepfather Jim's first wife died of a heart attack, he was wracked with pain over the "why." He searched for answers and wondered where God was. Through it all, Jim was able to keep his faith and it eventually deepened. For some, a crisis can turn them to God; for others, it can turn them from God. They feel abandoned.

The truth is that God is always with us, even in our pain.

Reverend Harold Kushner, who wrote *When Bad Things Happen to Good People,* says he believes that God does not control all that happens to us. Kushner believes there are laws in the Universe that God does not interfere with, although He set them in place. I believe one of these is the Law of Attraction. Kushner says we have a compassionate God, and when we have a loss, God grieves with us. I believe this also.

When my daughter died, I joined an infant loss support group. There were people in the group who felt abandoned by God, but there were many who saw God standing with them in their pain. In my experience, God was with me every step of the way. She protected me and softened the blows.

For instance, I chose to deliver my baby through natural childbirth, with no drugs, because of her fragile state. I wanted her to enter the world with no drugs in her system because she would immediately face three open-heart surgeries. As I labored in the high-risk birth room with a large team of doctors and nurses waiting for her arrival, all of us anticipated that the struggle for her life would begin after she left the safety of my womb. We were shocked to discover that she had died inside me. During the delivery, a heartbeat monitor clearly showed a heartbeat and looking at the monitor while I was in labor encouraged me that my hard work and labor without drugs were for her.

Afterward, the medical staff was puzzled by the equipment malfunction. They finally decided that, although they could not figure out how, the heartbeat monitor must have been showing my heartbeat. Had I known, too late into the painful labor to receive drugs, that my daughter had already died, I would not have had as much courage. This is just one example of the many times God was there with me during that difficult time.

Yes, tragedies occur. I am not going to write, like some teachers of the Law of Attraction do, that you attract every single bad thing that happens to you. I don't believe I created a baby with a severe heart defect or that she created that in my womb. I have a friend whose small child recovered from cancer, and as much as she believes in the Law of Attraction, her jaw tightens when she says her son did not attract his cancer, nor did she attract it to him.

I believe the Laws of the Universe are more complex than that. I believe that some things that happen to us we may contract as souls before we even enter our bodies.

I also believe in the Law of Polarity, or the Law of Opposites, which states we have to experience the full range of emotions to know them fully. In other words, to know light we must know dark. To know joy, we must know grief. This is our growth.

Part of being human is experiencing some loss. All things are changing and when things change, we feel loss, even if what we move on to is better. Trusting that God is here with us, and that we live in a benevolent Universe, allows us to relax into, and welcome, the next change.

GOD'S HAND AT WORK

When has God been there for you, even when Her hand seems hidden? Make a list.

It's Up to You

It is vital that we refuse to stay caught up in the loss. To do so would be like being wedged between rocks in the river of life. Or worse, to feel the loss so strongly that we try to wade upstream to recover something that is already gone from us.

Instead, turn and flow downstream. Fully experience the emotion and let it go so you can move to a higher emotion as a testament of love for yourself. The best way to do this is with support and healing from God. The source of the river and the support for your journey is your Source, who can help you turn and flow with grace downstream into the life you want.

When I listen to God, this is what I hear Her say:

People have dreams of falling. It scares them because falling means losing control and letting go of all the structures of ego and the beliefs they have built around themselves. What if one does fall, knowing only that I am there to catch them in the palm of my hand? Is that not a comforting thought? Instead of falling, it feels more like floating into my embrace.

CHAPTER 6

Receiving God

After years of being a hard-driving professional woman, I approached getting pregnant the same way. I was going to get pregnant through sheer willpower. I thought I could just order my body to get pregnant on command! When it didn't happen on schedule, I treated it like any other obstacle: I would roll right over it like a tank. In other words, I was going to force my way upstream again.

Because I was in rural southwest Virginia, my choices for fertility treatment were limited. I found a fertility doctor an hour away in Kingsport, Tennessee, and soon was driving there every day to get my blood drawn. My husband was taught to give me daily shots of high-octane fertility drugs and we eventually decided, after no success, to have an invasive surgery to place eggs and sperm inside my fallopian tubes.

The surgery required two weeks of bed rest, after which we returned to the doctor for a pregnancy test. We drove the hour with high expectations to see if I was pregnant. I knew I was. I could feel a baby girl's presence in me. But when they called us in the room, by the look on the nurse practitioner's face, I could tell it was bad news.

As she was telling me I wasn't pregnant, I had a voice inside me telling me something different. The voice said I was pregnant, and that the doctor would discover it in the afternoon after the qualitative analysis was done in the lab. The voice told me that the nurse would try desperately to get in touch with me to tell me I was pregnant and that I would not be available.

I didn't trust the voice assuring me I was pregnant. Crushed that I had gone through so much for no baby, I dissolved into tears. Once we got home, my husband, in an effort to cheer me up, suggested we go to our favorite Mexican restaurant. In resignation, I even ordered a beer. After running errands and grocery shopping, we returned home to find our answering machine blinking with several urgent messages from the doctor's office.

I called and they told me I was pregnant. The voice had come, the guidance was there—and yet I had refused to receive it.

Receiving is what life is really about. Receiving God, receiving yourself, and receiving direct guidance from God about how to manifest your life.

The primary dictionary definition of receiving is "to accept something given." Other definitions also relate: "take delivery of a message; greet, hear, or acknowledge something; and partake of the Communion." Having a relationship with God is all of these definitions, especially partaking of Communion with God. Every day God gives to us, we merely need to receive.

Refusing to Receive

We don't need to kneel at a railing and stick out our tongue like traditional Catholics receiving Communion. Instead we can receive the way the mystics do. Mystics are defined as those having direct communion with God. No one has to put a consecrated host on their tongue for them to have a direct experience with their Creator. Instead they open up to receive the fullest union with God. Initially, this was frightening to them, but as they surrendered to it, they were rewarded with ecstasy.

Mystics live their lives guided by God. They infuse their lives with God's Holy Spirit and they have the miracles to prove it. More important than the miracles is how direct communion with God changes them into people who live in the world but are not of it.

We all have mystical moments and divine guidance but most of us choose to reject the experience. As I sat in the doctor's office, listening to an expert tell me I was not pregnant, the greatest expert of all was telling me I was. And in my body and feelings (unlike the wild thoughts that come from my mind in a firestorm of chatter), I already knew it was true. I knew when I woke up that morning that I was pregnant with a little girl. I just had not developed faith in that voice. Too many times before, I had convinced myself I was pregnant with the sense that I could "iron will" it so.

I resisted the message in order to protect myself. Sometimes wanting something so badly hurts, so we dare not believe we will get it if there seems little chance. We want rock-solid proof that we are going to get it before we let ourselves open to the possibility. When my guidance told me I was pregnant, but the test said I was not, I did not want to get hurt. Although I heard it and in my bones I knew the pregnancy was true, "reality" was telling me something else.

I wonder how Mary felt when the Angel Gabriel came to her to tell her she was pregnant. She exclaimed, "it is impossible," and Gabriel reminded her that nothing is impossible with God.

"Reality" was telling her that there was NO WAY she could be pregnant. Imagine her fear of being an unmarried woman pregnant in that stern traditional culture. She must have had great apprehension when she told her fiancé Joseph that she was pregnant, since they both knew he was not the man who had impregnated her. Yet with great risk comes great rewards. She gave birth to Jesus and watched him change the world with his words and actions.

How many times have you had that wise voice talk to you, only to dismiss it? How many times was it signaling a great change in your life or warning you of danger? How many times have you later realized that it was the wisest counsel? Sometimes, at the moment, it doesn't fit with our logic, but in hindsight the guidance is right on. Often the voice is telling us that we stand on the threshold of a new life.

Blocked by Beliefs

There is a belief among many that God only speaks to a chosen few. This certainly is a view propagated by several major religions. In the past, to claim God spoke directly to you was blasphemy and the punishment for it was torture or death, especially during the Inquisition. It was believed that God spoke only to the rarified few, usually clergy, who were then qualified to interpret for the common people.

Mystics had to have proof that God had spoken to them. A common proof was to have a vision wherein the mystic was presented with a scroll, conferring a special dispensation for a direct relationship.

Requiring an interceder for God, instead of a direct relationship, is one of the main reasons that new churches broke from the Roman Catholic Church. Even the Holy Bible was protected as a text that only the clergy could interpret. When the printing press was invented, which enabled common people to own and read the Holy Bible, it shook the very foundation of the established church.

In our current time, having God speak directly to you raises questions about your mental health. Counselors are trained to be on the alert for people who speak of hearing God. At my church recently, a woman testified that she had heard God and had seen violet flames. When her boss noticed a change in her and asked what was going on and she shared her experience, this woman was referred to the Employee Assistance Program to be assessed for mental health problems.

Now granted, mentally ill people often do hear God talking to them and it can be a sign of a serious mental illness, but they usually have delusions and ego grandiosity as well. In the past thirty years, therapists have become much more overtly spiritual in their therapy practice and accepting of their clients' spirituality. Yet there is still concern about those who claim to talk to God.

All this can inhibit us as we start to receive the messages God sends us. Before we move forward, let's remove beliefs that might block our direct experience with God.

BLOCKED BY BELIEFS

What kind of clutter is blocking your direct experience with God? Do you believe God can speak directly to you ? Do you worry your mind is playing tricks on you? Do you feel you have to have proof other than your experience?

A Personal Relationship with God

An important linchpin to establishing any relationship is trust. If we don't trust that we will be safe, we enter into a relationship feeling out of balance. Often the most stressful relationships are when the power dynamic feels uneven. Can you trust that you will be safe with God? Can you trust that if you open your heart, you will not be disappointed again?

Are you really willing to receive the God you want into your life? Having a personal relationship with God may bring up some blocks for you. Maybe it is about being unworthy to have this relationship. Maybe it is because past religious exposure either encouraged or discouraged a personal relationship. Having a personal relationship is a topic that conservative Christians talk about a lot. When I move past my political bias, I find much wisdom in their discussion of it. The mystic in me resonates with the charismatic way they talk of God.

Handling Snakes

We all handle snakes in our search for God, but some handle more than just the metaphor. I was fascinated when I talked with Dennis Covington, the journalist who wrote *Salvation on Sand Mountain: Snake Handling and Redemption in Southern Appalachia,* a book about attending a snake-handling church. He began handling snakes himself because he felt it was a way to connect with God. Members of snake-handling churches believe that handling snakes while in rapture with God is an expression of trust and surrender.

We don't have to handle real snakes as an expression of trust and surrender. We just have to invite God in as we handle the dangers and perils of everyday life.

YOUR REPTILES

Some mystics have referred to the fears that surface in our life and block our relationship with God as reptiles. What kind of fears do you have about surrendering to a relationship with God? Are you afraid that if you do, you will not be able to function in the rough and tumble of the world?

Spiritual Hunger

Ever feel weak and listless, only to realize that you are far hungrier than you realized? Or have you felt sick, only to discover that you are dehydrated? Often not having God in your life is like this. Spiritual teachers compare the soul's yearning for God to being hungry or thirsty.

Often, people feel empty, dissatisfied, and restless. Like the person trying to quench his thirst with soda instead of water, or junk food instead of real nourishment, he is left lacking.

How do we become so distracted that we don't feel our hunger or thirst? Anyone who has a life crammed with too much to do recognizes this problem. When we most need to fuel our body is often when we forget it—until our body forces us to pay attention.

Our soul is like this. We may feel weak, lethargic, and disconnected, but unless there is a red flag flying, we don't recognize it. And when we do, it is easy to resist healthier alternatives when we most need them. Our body becomes so hungry that we reach for a quick and easy fix.

Spiritual yearning can be quenched only through Divine communion. For some, it can stay latent for years; for others, it bursts out uncontrollably. If you can admit your hunger, which you may have been covering up with other things, you are better able to receive God.

O God, thou art my God;
early will I seek thee:
my soul thirsteth for thee,
my flesh longeth for thee in a dry and thirsty land,
where no water is;

to see thy power and thy glory,
so as I have seen thee in the sanctuary.

Because thy loving-kindness is better than life,
my lips shall praise thee.

Thus will I bless thee while I live:
I will lift up my hands in thy name.

My soul shall be satisfied as with marrow and fatness.

—Psalm 63:1–5

Our soul's hunger is like this. We get so overwhelmed that we forget we are hungry. As a global community we regularly see disasters, wars, tsunamis, earthquakes, and hurricanes. The terror of events such as 9/11 brings human despair into our living rooms. We are assaulted daily by images of suffering. And everyday life feels harder.

Spiritual Nourishment

Finding the God you want is the answer to a more satisfying life. There is a great payoff for moving past your resistance and having your own conversation with God. Instead of being easily tossed about by the crisis of the day, you find a path to happiness.

People who have a spiritual life report higher levels of happiness and live longer lives. Study after study proves this. *Time* magazine's article "The Science of Happiness" by Claudia Wallis in January 2005, notes that "faith seems to genuinely lift the spirit." When people were asked, "What one thing in life has brought you the greatest happiness?" a relationship with God came in third, according to the article.

I have been fortunate that, for the most part, my experience with religion has been gentle, inspiring, and positive, but I know this is not the case with many people. I hear story after story of people hurt, angry, or damaged by their religious experience. They push against the God they don't want because they don't want to be hurt again. God was used against them. Yet they ache for connection and their hearts long to be filled. They have a hole in their heart that no amount of success, food, alcohol, or possessions will fill.

Splitting Ourselves

God's voice often comes to us in subtle ways and comes from *inside* us, although not solely from us. By putting God outside, we lose much of our direct connection with Her. In doing so, we cannot have the same power in the connection. When we hear a voice inside us, we doubt that it could be God. Sometimes the hesitancy in receiving God's guidance is thinking instead that it comes, simply, from our Highest Self. Yet God created this Highest Self.

So much of our pain stems from the illusion that we are separate from God. When we imagine that God is a separate entity in the sky, a man with a long flowing beard looking over his endless creations, it is easy to feel abandonment and loss. We feel like a child whom no one notices in a large family. We may feel like God does not care about our little lives.

We are not separate from God. God is in us, in all of us, and all around us. God is throughout us, outside of us, in every breath we take, in the food we eat, in the people we love, and even in the enemies we hate.

God is always here with us. We know His voice because it is the one of love. Learn to discern and have confidence that God is speaking to you.

Trusting God's Voice

I chose to dismiss the voice in the fertility doctor's office because it seemed to go against the reality of the situation. I rationalized that it was wishful thinking on my part, even though the voice did not feel like mine. I just wasn't able to trust it because I had not developed enough faith in it. Learning to honor God's voice can help guide us through all the situations in our lives.

Lauren, a friend of mine, was reminded of this recently while on a spiritual retreat where participants explored the truth in their lives. She felt like her feelings were a big pot of soup and she could not get any clarity. Then she looked up at the sky and said, "Please let me have something pop here. Please let me have clarity."

In an instant, she experienced a visible shift in energy and felt she was a little girl again, back in a home where she was often confused and did not have an adult she could go to for support. The truth of her current situation came to her and she realized she was not that little girl now and she could ask those around her for support and advice.

She clearly saw a solution to her problem and was aware of a belief system that had been blocking her progress. She asked for guidance and was answered in a way that she could not ignore; yet later she said she did not appreciate how often she receives guidance like that.

I have heard this voice many times. Most of the time it sounds like MY voice in my head and yet it is wiser, clearer, and more concise. I know deep in my psyche that it is not my voice. I remember once working with a much younger woman on a project and being upset about some dynamics at work. Just as I was about to say something that would have caused me professional problems, I heard a voice tell me to "be very careful." I was vibrating with nervous defensive energy and who knows what I might have unleashed in the other woman. She was close with my superiors and, due to her youth, may not have been discreet.

ARE YOU TALKING TO ME?

Let's look at your belief systems about God's talking to you. What have you been told about God talking directly to people? Where did you get this? How does this make you feel? List any unease you have.

Feeling the Voice of God

In all the research I have done on receiving God's guidance and learning how to access the Divine, the one unified thing I have come across is how God's messages make people FEEL. These messages come in without much emotion and are clear. God is the still, quiet voice inside that guides us. His voice does not have the same flavor as the self-talk we give ourselves, which is full of worry, fear, and self-criticism. Instead, His voice instructs us with a gentle power and authority.

Of course, there is resistance to talking directly with God. It is scary. It makes one doubt. And yet when you learn to accept it, it feels more real than anything else in your life. It is like putting on a pair of glasses that allows you to see new dimensions. Like X-ray glasses that allow you to see through what is considered "reality" and find the truth underneath.

I will ask the Father, and he will give you another Counselor to be with you forever—the Spirit of Truth. The world cannot accept him, because it neither sees him nor knows him. But you will know him, for he lives with you and will be in you.

—John 14:16–17

Resisting the Feeling of God

We resist not only God's guidance, but also the intensity that comes with God. To receive a gift so precious, so profound, so amazing feels like too much for us to bear. It brings up fears about strength and surrender.

Issues of strength come up because we worry we may not be strong enough to have direct connection with God. Often we resist God to protect ourselves. God feels too big, too awesome, too much to grasp. Opening into God can feel a little bit like falling into a void. It can be scary. The feeling is blissful but it *is* intense. We wonder if we are strong enough to sustain Divine communion. We fear we may lose ourselves.

The first time I remember feeling bliss and fear about God's power was when I was eleven. I was staying at a lodge with my family at a conference my father had organized. I had two playmates and we formed a secret club. We were playing at magic and we had decided to fly like fairies. I remember running across the grass with them at dusk, all holding hands and feeling like we really were taking off from the ground. My feet were no longer on the grass. I become one with the air and my friends. I disappeared and merged with all around me. For a moment, I did not exist.

I am convinced in retrospect that I was having some kind of mystical experience, but it scared me silly. Each of us knew something supernatural had happened. We each wore a small plastic ring on our finger to represent our magic and membership in our club. I took mine off (and never put it back on) and suggested that we play another game. All three of us looked shaken and never mentioned it again. The feeling was so profound that to this day I have kept that little blue plastic ring. It sits in my jewelry box to remind me of that experience.

RESISTING BLISS

Think back to when you experienced bliss. Did it feel too much for you to handle? Have you had a mystical experience that felt overwhelming? What might allow you to handle this intensity better?

Will I Lose Me?

One fear is that we will lose ourselves. Spiritual teachers tell us that this is a good thing. The Sufis urge us to let our ego fall away and merge with the Divine. Buddhists aspire to enlightenment and Nirvana; they say the ultimate experience is nothingness. Mystics talk about the bliss of Divine union. Many Christians testify about the power of being born again, a term that implies that all you were has been transformed into a new life. Yet despite the many spiritual traditions that sing the praises of merging with God and remind us that we are never separate from God, losing oneself is a scary thought. It can make us feel weak and vulnerable.

What comes up for me is that it took me a long time to *find* myself. I spent so much time merging with the people I loved in my life that often I had trouble remembering who I was. I finally found myself and felt my own identity, not dependent on others. On my journey to God, I discovered that one of my barriers is that I have resistance to losing myself again after having just found myself.

Merging into God can bring up feelings of merging with our mothers. Sometimes, just as the mother relationship can feel overwhelming, this brings up the same feelings of fear.

As an older elementary school child, I felt overwhelmed by my mother. She was trying so hard to be a good mother, yet I felt so overpowered by her. I used to wish she would get a job so the focus would not be so fixed on me. As her only daughter, we were tightly merged and I had trouble sensing where I started and she ended. I used to run for the school bus each morning feeling my lungs contracting because I felt so smothered. Once I was on the bus, my lungs would relax and I could take a deep breath.

These feelings were reactivated through spiritual work. When I was in a deep state while working with my spiritual teacher, all of a sudden it felt like my heart was leaping out of my body, trying to merge with the Divine. For a minute I felt joy and bliss, but then a strong fear arose and I pulled back. I was afraid to merge with the Divine because, again, I feared I would lose myself. As delicious as the merging was, it was scary. I had been in bliss, where I felt I wanted to be, but I pulled back.

What I had not considered is that I cannot lose myself in God because I am never separate from God. Although merging may have brought up scary feelings for me, the reality was blissful.

Divine Union through Sex

Speaking of bliss, the closest most of us come to merging with God is through sex. It is the one time many people feel like they have touched God. It is certainly a time when many people call out to God!

Sexual pleasure can bring up these same fears. Sexual release is all about letting go of control. In discussions with other women, I discovered that sometimes women resist orgasm because it means giving up their power. Many times in my twenties, I felt this fear come up while making love with my husband. I would hold back from melting into the pleasure because I was so afraid of letting go.

For most of us, as we age, we realize the power of letting go, both in climax and in life. There are great rewards for giving up control and tearing down the walls we have built.

True strength comes when you allow yourself to be vulnerable. Whether it is merging into a partner's love or Divine communion, bliss comes from surrendering.

Surrendering to God

Surrender is a term that brings up lots of baggage for most people. When a client has boundary issues or fears conflict, we work together to move them into a warrior archetype. A warrior sets strong boundaries and defends his territory. It seems contradictory to advise surrender when I teach so many people how to be more like warriors. Yet warriors, from the Japanese Samurai to the Amazons, pledge their allegiance to a leader. They surrender their control to a higher power.

In the Native American tradition, the search for meaning usually starts with an initial quest for a guiding vision. Alone in the wilderness, each seeker exposes himself to unknown forces without any protection. He patiently waits for a message from the Great Spirit that will determine his future course. As a spiritual warrior, he surrenders completely.

Surrender was a hard concept for me to learn. I had a successful career in politics, charging ahead and making things happen. I came right out of college and got a job in the governor's office in Virginia, and moved my way up, from campaigns to government for three governors, until my political party got thrown out and there were no jobs for Democrats in the state capital. Even then I landed on my feet and became a campaign manager for a congressman in southwest Virginia. I was successful because I did not surrender. I plowed over obstacles and moved mountains, often working late into the night.

Surrender felt to me like failure. But I came to learn that real surrender is victory. I learned how to surrender when my child died. By giving up an intense push for an outcome and letting God know what I wanted, I was given my other children. I realized the value in surrender and embraced it. I started to live my life asking for outcomes, holding intentions, but surrendering to how they would arrive in my life. And if my intention did not manifest, I asked myself what I needed to change about myself, or if I was being protected by not getting what I wanted.

As I watched others who were like me, it helped me see how sometimes surrender to the highest outcome is the wisest course of action. While I was in the governor's office, I watched a young woman become obsessed with getting into the University of Virginia's law school. Because she wanted it so desperately and pushed so hard, I saw her repel admission further and further away. She had been turned down once and yet year after year she made another run at getting admitted. She badgered the admissions office and compiled letters of recommendation from people prominent in government. Instead of acknowledging there were other good law schools, or seeing the rejection as a sign to move on, she kept charging single-mindedly ahead. I was sitting with her once when she called the admissions office and I could tell from the way the conversation was going that her pushing had so angered the staff that there was no way she was going to get in. She had pushed them into resisting her admission.

Receiving Is about Surrendering

Receiving is about surrendering. About understanding that we are able to point ourselves in the right direction and see where we want to end up, but then trusting that God will bring us there. When we have a bumpy ride, it is time to let God take over the reins.

During tough times, remember the promise of Psalm 18:

> *I love you, O Lord, with all my strength.*
> *The Lord is my rock, my fortress, and my deliverer;*
> *my God is my rock, in whom I take refuge.*
> *He is my shield and the horn of my salvation,*
> *My stronghold.*

Surrender may feel like the opposite of the Law of Attraction. It is a paradox, but all spiritual laws are in paradox. Many teachers emphasize that, although you work to attract what you want by thinking, feeling, visioning, and receiving, an important key is relaxing so that the right outcome will occur. The Universe is fluid, constantly changing, and there are so many unseen factors. Part of our job is to let go. It is to surrender to the outcome. It is to see that God always has our best interests at heart.

God put the Law of Attraction in place, but She also likes to surprise Her Children. If you ask for something, God can make it much bigger, much grander than what you were expecting.

PART TWO

Create Your Life with God

Chapter 7

Making the Overture

As a child, I always prayed, but it never dawned on me that God could carry on a two-way conversation with me. I knew only that He commanded in the Bible and that I had the choice to answer yes or no to His directives. Prayer was always a one-way street. I would beg, all the while believing God's answer would be in whether or not I got what I prayed for.

I was in college when I first heard a voice respond to me and my reaction was disbelief. I had been praying for guidance about my love life while on a first date with a man who had already swept me off my feet. Before we left the car to go into the restaurant, he leaned over and kissed me. As I walked into the restaurant, I was reeling, drunk with love.

At that moment, a voice said to me, "You will love this man but do not marry him."

Throughout the whole relationship I remembered this, despite his discussions of marriage and my mother's consternation that I would not consider this man a good catch.

On the outside he looked perfect—intelligent, handsome, and from an established family who adored me. His father was prominent in government and he had a warm mother I could love as my own. Eventually, it became clear to me why I could not marry him, no matter how much I loved him. He was harshly critical and often put me down in public settings.

Over the years, our families have remained friends and his life is different from what I would have chosen for myself. He has been married twice, has no children, and suffers from depression.

I was attracting this man into my life as a mate. Since I have a pattern of relationships in which I am criticized and devalued, I am grateful I was spared having more than one ex-husband because I was blessed with such strong guidance. Clearly, I was on my way to creating trouble had I not had an intervention!

God usually requires that we make the overture. When we do and listen alertly, we are rewarded. Sometimes the gift is a word or a sentence that guides us. Sometimes it is a calmness that washes over us. But we can't receive it if we don't ask for it. We have to make the overture.

I will speak to you if you will listen. I will come to you if you will invite Me. I will show you then that I have always been there. All ways.

—Neale Donald Walsch, *Conversations with God, Book 1,* page 58

Put Your Toe in the Water

So it is time to try. Time for you to make an overture to God that is deliberate and focused. Time for you to make an advance in a way that is conscious and mindful. Time for you to try when there's no crisis brewing in your life.

You may already practice a prayer or meditation routine. You may already talk to God. If so, work at bringing a different energy to the conversation. Work at being relaxed, joyful, and full of gratitude. Begin a new spiritual practice with anticipation and discipline.

For those of you who haven't prayed much, you may be stumped on how to begin. Elizabeth Gilbert writes in *Eat, Pray, Love* that she began her first conversation by saying, "Hi, God. It's me, Liz." Your conversation can be that simple. Although I giggled when I read the way Elizabeth made her overture to God, I also liked it. It was said the way we might greet a new friend. God doesn't need pleasantries, but if you are going to start having conversations like you do with other people, instead of just during crisis times, then why not proceed as though you are talking to a friend?

Adding God to Every Equation

For those of you who have some experience in making an approach to God, take it a step further. Try stretching yourself; if you have a regular time to pray or meditate, then stretch into integrating God throughout your entire day.

One thing I have found helpful is to say a prayer right before I do something important, such as a coaching session or a workshop. I always ask that God move through me, guide me, and help me serve those with whom I am working.

I advocate adding God to every equation. I found that it has made a profound difference in how I live my life. The way I connect with God most intensely is through the Holy Spirit. All through my day I ask the Holy Spirit to be with me. I feel this presence acutely while I am working. I start each coaching session with a silent request for the Holy Spirit to be at my side. If, during a session, a client is emotional or stumped, or I am unsure in which direction to go, I ask the Holy Spirit for guidance. Invariably, I know the right questions to ask or words of wisdom will arise that will help my client. I know, in those moments, that what happened did not come from me but rather *through* me. I ask for the Holy Spirit's guidance when I write, whether it is a sensitive email, a speech, or a chapter in a book.

I find it particularly helpful as I parent my children. Often my clients have an idealized view of me as a calm Zen-like mother who never yells and always knows the right answer. Nothing could be further from the truth. For me, being a conscious spiritual person who stays mindful and present in the moment is most challenged when I parent.

I have wonderful children whom I adore. Yet they are a handful. They bring out the best and worst in me. They have spent years watching their father be disrespectful to me so sometimes they repeat what they have had modeled for them. I catch myself in an old pattern of shutting down when this happens.

One daughter is particularly dramatic and used to throw herself to the floor in a nuclear meltdown when she felt out of control. The strength and fury in her tantrums pushed all my old buttons of being afraid of people in a rage. During these challenging moments, if I can REMEMBER to ask God for help, I seem to know what to do.

Adding God to every equation is not something that usually occurs spontaneously for me. I consider it part of my spiritual practice, a discipline that I have to focus on in order to remember. For me it is a mindfulness practice: to be present enough to remember to ask God in. I work to remember to ask God into my life throughout my day, whether I am crossing a street, driving through town, or shopping at a grocery store. My day goes more smoothly and I glide through the hours feeling wrapped in God's grace.

When my clients want to change something in their lives, sometimes if they seem open, I'll suggest that they try asking God to assist them in the effort.

A press secretary wanted to increase his confidence during press conferences. I asked him if he had ever considered asking for God's help in improving his performance—right before the press conference began. He had a personal relationship with God and was a committed churchgoer but he had never considered bringing God into a work task. He found that when he did so, he felt a presence with him as he answered questions. His confidence and ability to focus quickly increased.

The same experience happened to a woman I coached who taught a children's music class. She is a talented musician and teacher. She realized if she started each class with a silent prayer for God to work through her and a request that she best serve her children, her classes were even more successful.

I am friends with a fellow coach who suffers from migraine headaches. Her spiritual practice inspires me and conversations with her have helped deepen my spirituality. But like all of us, she had not thought to ask God into certain aspects of her life. One day when we were talking about her migraines, I questioned whether she had asked God for a healing. She paused, a little startled by the question, and admitted that she had not thought of asking God directly for a healing.

Reverend Stretton Smith felt the same way about ringing in his ears. He tells the story of how he spent lots of money going to specialists only for them to come back to him and tell him he had ringing in his ears (which he already knew) and that it was incurable. For years he did not consider asking for a healing, until one day he sat on a log and said, "Thank you, God, for healing the ringing in my ears." He heard a large pop and the ringing in his ears stopped. Although it came back twice more, a prayer giving thanks for healing cured him both times.

I heard a similar story from the young lawyer who handled my house financing. She had been suffering from fibromyalgia and fibroid tumors. Her doctor said she needed to have surgery for the tumors, but even that measure would not ensure that she would be healthy. She was in a state of chronic pain and exhaustion. A devout Christian, she realized one day while driving to work that a test of her faith would be believing God could heal her. She said, "God, I have faith in you and believe you will heal me." After saying this, she was shocked to see a puff of white smoke come out of her mouth. Her symptoms disappeared and her doctor could find no further problems.

These people were suffering from problems and didn't realize that they could invite God into their life to help them. Sometimes God sends us a full healing; at other times, God grants us access to resources such as the latest advances in medicine.

LETTING GOD IN EVERYWHERE

What places in your life have you not considered letting God in? Think about inviting God into every part of your life.

Reconnecting with God

I am the beginning of your first thought. I am the end of your last. I am the idea which sparked your most brilliant moment. I am the glory of its fulfillment. I am the feeling which fueled the most loving thing you ever did. I am the part of you which yearns for that feeling again and again.

Whatever works for you, whatever makes it happen— whatever ritual, ceremony, demonstration, meditation, thought, song, word, or action it takes for you to "reconnect"—do this. Do this in remembrance of Me.

—Neale Donald Walsch, *Conversations with God, Book 2,* page 26

In this quote, we are given guidance on how to *reconnect* with God. It is a reminder that we have always had a connection with God, we merely need to renew that relationship. We are given ways to reconnect: ritual, ceremony, demonstration, meditation, thought, song, word, and action. Think about all the many ways you can make an overture. What way speaks to you?

Can you have a ritual in which you light a candle and ask God more fully into your life? Can you do a ceremony with your family to bless your home and ask God to reside there with you? Can you demonstrate your new relationship with God by dedicating some action, perhaps your next walk or run, to it? Can you start a daily meditation practice for just five minutes a day? Can you try to have a thought about God once an hour? Can you sing a hymn or a rousing gospel song? Or even come up with your own chant in honor of your special relationship with God? Can you, like the Sufi poet Rumi, write a love poem to God? Can you stop and help another and tell God that you did it in remembrance of Her?

Pick a way that speaks to you. Relationship therapists say people show love differently. Some people use words to show their love, others their creative talents. Many people use work to show love because they have trouble expressing it with words. Make your own overture in the way that works for you.

Take Baby Steps

We all get the jitters when we first talk to God. The most important thing for you to do is take some baby steps. Try these basic steps:

1. Quiet yourself.
2. Ask God in.
3. Express gratitude.
4. Share, or ask for guidance.
5. Listen.

The key is to ask God to come in and then be ready for an answer. You can say "hello" or simply say the lines from the religious hymn, "Here I am, Lord."

LETTER FROM GOD
Close your eyes and ask for God to make Herself known. Open your eyes and write a letter from God to yourself. What does God tell you?

A Joyful Noise

Since I was a child, I have loved the contemporary hymn with the lyrics "Make a joyful noise unto the Lord." God wants to hear from us when we are grateful and happy. Of course, God is with us in crisis, but just like our family, He doesn't want to hear from us only when we are in trouble.

Far too often, we turn to God only when we are in crisis and then we stay stuck in our "don't wants" and run right up against the Law of Attraction. Don't spend your time with God whining and complaining. Express gratitude. Don't pray about what you don't want. Ask for what you *do* want. Share what you want God to know about your life. Yes, yes, God already knows everything, but She appreciates a good conversation.

With the possible exception of prayer, which is more often a plea from a closed rather than opened valve, precious few of us were ever taught to go inside, shut up and listen, much less follow! Follow what? Listen to whom?

—Lynn Grabhorn, *Excuse Me, Your Life Is Waiting,* page 168

Quieting Down

In the hustle and bustle of everyday life, having some time set aside to establish the spiritual discipline of communicating with God means that we are open enough to hear what is coming to us.

Be still, and know that I am God.

—Psalm 46:10

Mystics through the ages have known this. They retreated from life so that they could move forward with God. Moses went on top of the mountain. Jesus went into the desert. Buddha sat under the Bodhi tree. Mohammad went into a cave. Monks and nuns go to monasteries. For some, even a monastery does not offer enough solitude. Certain monks and nuns receive special permission to live in huts deep in the woods.

Many cultures have a hermit or sacred man who withdraws from society to commune with God in nature. Indian mystics are especially well known for their tendency to live in caves or in the jungle. In India, there is even a tradition that middle-class men who have raised their families and had successful careers take a year to go and live the life of a wandering holy man.

Although the tradition of seeking solitude is more honored in the East, there are many in the West who seek it out. Throughout the ages, Christian mystics have withdrawn from society to draw closer to God. Even those that we don't think of as mystics but who inspire us lived the mystic's path for a while. Thoreau had Walden Pond. Emily Dickinson retreated to her room. Carlos Castaneda went into the desert with don Juan. Ram Dass, Jack Kornfield, and many young Westerners lived in ashrams to learn wisdom from a guru.

Pema Chödrön, a Buddhist nun, inspires us with her writings from an abbey in Nova Scotia. Thich Nhat Hanh, the Vietnamese monk who has written the classic *Living Christ, Living Buddha,* has an ashram in France. Meditative communities and retreat centers abound. The thriving business of the Omega Institute and Esalen Institute in the United States is evidence of this thirst for quietude.

To write this book, I had to withdraw from my busy life. I am a social butterfly and an extrovert, yet I had to have solitude in order to write words that might have relevant meaning. With the demands of raising my children, running my own business, being a leader in various organizations, and having a rich social life with many interests, I found that I had to cut out all but the most essential priorities. Each time my children went to spend time with their father, I packed up my car and drove over the mountains, deep into the backwoods, to a cabin that was so remote that I had to ford a stream and climb a rough rugged road to get there. I went for days on end without talking to anyone, and the longer I was alone there the more I could hear what I was supposed to say.

Attar, the Sufi mystic, calls this quieting down "mystic silence" and praised it in a poem:

> *From each, Love demands a mystic silence.*
> *What do all seek so earnestly? 'Tis Love.*
> *Love is the subject of their inmost thoughts,*
> *In Love no longer "Thou" and "I" exist,*
> *For self has passed away in the Beloved.*
> *Now will I draw aside the veil from Love,*
> *And in the temple of mine inmost soul*
> *Behold the Friend, Incomparable Love.*
> *He who would know the secret of both worlds*
> *Will find that the secret of them both is Love.*

Mystic Silence in Modern Times

Most of us are not monks or nuns. In fact, I have shared with you my great fear as a child that God would insist I be a nun. We have chosen to live our lives in the world and still establish a relationship with God. The name given to people on the spiritual path who live in the world and carry responsibilities is a "householder." The focus of the spiritual teacher and mystic Gurdjieff was on self-awareness during the daily life of a householder and on humanity's place in the Universe.

The Diamond Approach Work believes that although the householder has greater challenges in being able to focus on the spiritual path, there are greater rewards to living a spiritual life that is in the world but not of it.

Jack Kornfield speaks eloquently of this in his book *A Path with Heart*. He talks of coming home to the United States from an ashram in India and realizing that true spiritual strength comes from being able to keep up one's practices and stay centered in the midst of life. He found it easy to do his practices and keep his balance in a quiet ashram, yet it is more real to be able to do so while in the world. He continued this theme of living the life of a householder in *After the Ecstasy, the Laundry*, a title that aptly describes the challenge.

Caroline Myss argues that there is a growing trend toward the modern mystic and she has named people committed to this path as "mystics without monasteries."

> **To be a mystic without a monastery means that you make a conscious decision to stop being motivated by fear— fear that you don't have enough, that you have to have more to meet your basic needs. And you replace fear with faith and compassion. In effect, you become a powerful instrument of God's grace. Infused with a force greater than our own—a divine intention, assistance, or insight that is spiritually rejuvenating—grace is energy that can fill you with a luminous awareness different from everyday consciousness. It motivates your spirit and lights your path from within.**
>
> —Caroline Myss, *Entering the Castle*, pages 36–37

The modern mystic is an individual who lives in the world but still desires a direct relationship with God. This may be a new trend in the West, but other cultures support those who aspire for a connection with the Divine while living the life of a householder. One example is in Tibet where every action is framed in relationship to the Divine.

As you start to grow your relationship with God, you have many models to follow. The householder or modern mystic is one that might suit your life best. Although large blocks of quiet time allow you to go deeper, mystic silence can be cultivated minute to minute. It can be a brief time—ten minutes in the morning and ten minutes at night—used to center and ground yourself.

MEDITATION MINUTE

Take one minute right now to clear your mind and close your eyes. Breathe in joy and breathe out suffering. Give joy a color as it comes into your body. Give suffering a color as it leaves your body. If your mind wanders, just gently bring it back to the breath.

Prayer

Prayer is a word that might bring up resistance in you. Often prayer is a rote recitation of words done with no feeling or mindfulness. Step away from the prayers you may have used since childhood. Search for other prayers that inspire and ignite you. They can be the words in a song, the poems of Rumi, the *Tao Te Ching,* the psalms in the Holy Bible, or from a book designed for daily devotion.

Often, moving outside your spiritual tradition and finding prayers that are different helps shake you out of the routine prayers that have become pointless for you. The different perspective, whether Hindu, Muslim, Buddhist, Native American, or a different Christian tradition, may awaken you and produce intense feelings as you pray. As you start to pray with love, devotion, and enthusiasm, you can return to prayers from your tradition with a new appreciation.

Free-form prayer is another way to stay engaged throughout the experience. You pray with your own thoughts and feelings, which is a powerful way to pray. You can do this in the morning or evening, or to bless food before you eat. You can also bless those around you, your family, your friends, your colleagues, and even enemies. The simple sentence "God bless you" when someone sneezes can be a real blessing rather than just an unthinking cliché.

All spiritual traditions urge us to pray for others. The Buddhists have a heart-centered meditation called *tong lin* practice, used to cultivate compassion for all sentient beings. In this practice, they allow compassion and love to expand and embrace it all, whatever it might be, without judgment.

As you pray, remember to stay in your power and come from a place of thanks and gratitude.

Decrees and Centering Prayer

Decrees are a form of prayer said aloud that claim and affirm our connection with God and our Highest Self. Every morning and evening, I say violet flame decrees from the book *Violet Flame to Heal Body, Mind, and Soul* by Elizabeth Clare Prophet. I say the decrees not only for myself, but also for my children, my friends, my family, and those with whom I'm in conflict.

The violet flame decrees raise our vibrations. The simplest decree *"I am a being of violet light, I am the purity that God desires"* is said while visualizing a violet flame burning away all negativity. I recommend Prophet's pocket-sized book filled with decrees and visualizations to help connect daily with God and purify your energy.

Centering prayer, which is similar to a mantra, uses a short phrase like "I love God with all my heart and soul" or merely "God" or "love." One word or a short phrase can be used repeatedly like a mantra to keep your mind focused and produce heat in your heart.

You can find your own centering prayer or work with a spiritual director to discover it. A guru often gives mantras.

Many people find chanting to be powerful. For some, chanting in Sanskrit, Tibetan, or Latin keeps them focused on the feeling rather than the words. The word "Om" is considered the universal sound. It is a sound so soothing that when my son was three and having tubes put in his ears, he asked me to chant it to him while he was going under anesthesia.

Prayer Can Dance through Your Day

Find ways to integrate prayer into your day. Instead of seeing it as a heavy obligation, imagine prayer as a mystical being that dances through your day and raises you up to dance with it.

I try to link prayer to specific actions so that I can more easily remember them. Because I want to honor my spiritual tradition, I say the "Our Father" and the "Hail Mary" while I make my bed. I start each morning with some violet flame decrees and a prayer for protection before I move into meditation. I end each day with violet flame decrees. For just a few minutes, I review my day and ask myself if there is anyone I need to forgive before I go to sleep. I don't want to carry old resentment and anger into my new day. Then I think of the ways God has blessed me during the day and I give thanks.

Prayers for Thanks

I believe that giving thanks and providing protection are the two most important ways to pray. Each night as I tuck my children in, I ask them to tell something for which they are grateful that God provided for them that day. Then I ask them to tell me something they are grateful for in the future, and we give thanks to God for it as if it were already here. We end with a recitation of the violet flame decrees.

A natural place in the day to give thanks and connect through prayer is before eating. While I was growing up, my family had a tradition of singing a prayer before dinner. Many believe that saying a blessing before we eat infuses the food with more nourishment.

Prayers and Whitewater

Many of us have prayed for protection when we face a threat. My most vivid memory is when I casually agreed to go whitewater rafting with a boyfriend. The day before we went, it began to dawn on me that I had agreed to something much more dangerous than I intended. This intensified when I discovered that my first experience would be to navigate Class V rapids, ranked as some of the roughest. By the time I was in the boat, my mind was filled with visions of people seriously injured or even killed. The rafting staff warned us that if we were swept out of the boat, we could get pulled under rocks and drown or we could become wedged in between rocks.

As a single mother with no health insurance, I started to realize that the consequences of getting hurt could be severe. Plus I wear hard contact lenses and if they were washed out of my eyes, I would be virtually blind.

My boatmates assured me that I needed to accept that I would probably be thrown from the boat. I look back on the DVD of that day and I can see from the quickness of my walk and the tightness of my face that I was terrified.

I spent the whole river trip in prayer. Every time we hit rough water, I thanked God for keeping me safe, in the boat, and connected to my contacts. I was able to relax some, although I didn't really enjoy myself.

After lunch, we faced our toughest rapids. Our boat ended up entering the whitewater askew so that we were swept right into a rock. Two people were thrown from the boat. The boat was upended and my face came within two feet of hitting a large rock before I used my paddle to push myself away from it. My skull could easily have been broken or my face disfigured. One of the men thrown from the boat broke his ankle.

Yet after the accident, I was calm and relaxed. I could have been hurt but I hadn't been. I had been protected. Looking back, I would have rather not had to pray so fervently for protection about a situation I had willingly entered into, but regardless, God was there for me.

Starting Your Day with Protection

Although we have all prayed for protection at one time or another, many people are unaware that there are specific prayers for protection. These prayers for protection not only keep us physically safe, but they also protect our energy from being punctured or drained by people who wish to harm or use us. We all know energy vampires, who wish to either penetrate our energy field or feed off it. When we are with them we feel drained. These prayers of protection are visualizations—of a tube of light, large crystal, or bubble or placing a rose between other people and you—that create a barrier around your energy field.

Over the years, I have taught hundreds of people a Native American prayer for protection. I learned it from my Shamanism teacher, Sue Wolfstar, but I have also found it in books attributed to the Navahos.

Visualize a beautiful rose with velvety petals.
Give your rose a color.
Appreciate the beauty of the rose and then notice
*   its strong stem with sharp thorns.*
Visualize the rose over your head. Say to yourself
"Beauty is above me."
Visualize a second rose under your feet. Say to yourself
*   "Beauty is beneath me."*
Visualize a third rose in front of you. Say to yourself
*   "Beauty is in front of me."*

Visualize a fourth rose behind you. Say to yourself
   "Beauty is behind me."
Visualize roses to the right and left of you. Say to yourself
   "Beauty is to the right and left of me."
Visualize roses all around you. See yourself surrounded by
   roses like you are in the middle of a rose thicket or large
   rose bush.
Feel how protected your energy feels. How if someone were
   to look at you with spiritual sight, they would see roses
   but if they were to try to reach in to harm you, the
   thorns would protect you.
      Say to yourself "Beauty is all around me."
Feel how protected your energy now feels.
Breathe into that feeling of safety.
End the prayer saying
   "I am ready and willing to face the day."

This prayer has a profound effect on people. I get calls and emails
all the time from clients and friends about the power this prayer has
in their life. Sometimes people will use it right before they go into a
stressful meeting, other times people will use it before seeing a family member who is cruel or draining. I taught it to one of my daughter's classmates who has an unkind stepfather. From children to
seniors, from CEOs to laborers in a manufacturing plant, and even
entire workshops—this prayer has made a huge difference in people's lives. I always feel protected when I say it.

PROTECTED BY PRAYER

Take a moment to say the Navaho prayer for protection and
visualize the roses around you. See yourself in the middle
of the rose thicket. Feel the space around you protected.

Prayer as Power

Prayer can change our lives. It can be used in times when we are
desperate and in the dark night of our soul. God will be there for us.
Yet I urge you to use it in a joyous way as well, a way of celebrating
and praising your connection to God.

Perhaps just as important as finding the image of God you want, you need to find the prayer you want. Maybe you feel resistance arising to the word "prayer." Claim the word and make it yours. Discover a prayer that speaks to you. Come up with your own prayers.

Contemplation

Contemplation is quiet reflection and thoughtful consideration. It often occurs after reading something that inspires or provokes us to consider a new way of thinking. Sacred texts offer powerful forms for contemplation. The Holy Bible, the Bhagavad-Gita, the Koran, the *Tao Te Ching*, *A Course in Miracles*, and Sufi translations are all feasts for contemplation. I also find the writings of Thich Nhat Hanh, Pema Chödrön, Eckhart Tolle, and Alan Watts rich in meaning. The founder of the Diamond Approach Work, A. H. Almaas, has written more than twenty books and his ideas prompt contemplation. The key to the work is to read and then reflect on how the meaning applies to your life.

A scripture that is not read with sincerity soon becomes covered with dust.

—*The Teaching of Buddha*, page 374

CONTEMPLATE WISDOM

Find a short section from a sacred text that appeals to you or even a quote from one of the teachers cited in this book. Read it carefully, reflecting on the word choice and meaning. After reading it twice, consider how this wisdom applies to your life.

Meditation

I need my daily morning meditation to start my day like some people need coffee. When I miss it, I feel like I am not operating as well that day. I am not as open to messages. Without meditation, it is harder for me to hold my center when faced with a problem or affected by the emotions of others.

Meditation helps us keep our vibrations higher so that we can attract what we want. It gives us time to visualize what we want in our life and feel it coming in. In *The Secret*, Rhonda Byrne says that every great teacher she interviewed about the Law of Attraction meditated every day.

Most people tell me they are too busy to meditate. They see it as a problem to fit into their life, instead of a wonderful gift to give to themselves. They tell me all the reasons they can't do it, perhaps because their inner critic tells them they have to do it the "right way" and devote large blocks of time to it. Any time can ground you and help smooth your day. As the mom of three active young children, I don't want to hear the excuses. On weekdays, I meditate for about ten minutes. I set my alarm just a little earlier and do it in bed. On weekends, I take longer.

I don't ever want meditation to be something that makes my children feel separate from me, so they often join me if they are quiet. Sometimes they sit in my lap. Sometimes they bring me an object from my altar and put it in my hand. They have learned it is something important to me and it has become part of their routine as well as mine.

My most creative ideas are generated from this meditative experience. I don't worry so much about all the mind chatter, except when it keeps me too disengaged from the meditating. Instead, I work on feeling my body, feeling energy flowing through my body, and giving thanks for what I want in my life, in advance. When I notice that I have followed a train of thought or gotten distracted, I just gently return to my meditation.

I also guide my children in meditation, although this is sometimes challenging! More successful is a short prayer or visualization and then have them think of a joint goal we have as a family and have them thank God in advance for this. They love thinking of our family as a visioning team to attract a better life for all of us.

Even very small children are open to a short meditation. When my kids were little, I used to be the substitute teacher in their pre-

MINI MEDITATION

Feel your feet grounded on the earth. Breathe deeply. Gently ask your mind to quiet.

Imagine the sun all around you. As you start to breathe, pull a golden liquid from the sun into your body. Feel the warmth pool in your belly and flow through your veins. Visualize your whole body being filled with a warm melted golden sun. Relax into the feeling.

school. Kids as young as two years old were able to do a short guided meditation. A classroom of two-year-olds would lie on their backs, seeing the sun shining inside them and growing a flower in their bellies. I fully believe that if two-year-olds can do it, you can, too.

Chattering Monkeys

Eastern meditation practices often talk of monkey mind, in which our minds are filled with chattering monkeys. I like to think of turning down the volume on them or moving those chattering monkeys to the background. Stephen Levine has beautiful guided meditations in which he talks about thoughts resembling shooting stars that you only notice and don't need to follow. Even experienced meditation teachers admit that they must come back to the meditation repeatedly. The discipline to return to quiet is worth the effort

Recently, I was at a coach meeting where one of our colleagues was demonstrating a meditation technique she uses with clients. She talked about the importance of not resisting chatter in the mind, but simply not letting it dominate. One coach had never heard that it was okay to have mind chatter. She said she thought there was something wrong with her and it was a relief to hear that most people struggle with this and that it is okay. For the first time, she realized it was fine to allow the experience she was having instead of struggling with it.

It is essential to remember that what you resist persists. So if you put your energy and attention into resisting all the mind chatter, it merely grows bigger. Relax with it. Let the chatter sit in the room with you like a noisy relative you give little attention to. Just don't give it much focus. And when you do, calmly redirect your mind, the way you might remind a child who has gone astray.

Opening Your Heart

As you struggle with your mind in meditation, it is helpful to remember your heart. A powerful way to make an overture to God is to open your heart to Her. Feeling into your heart space while praying, meditating, or doing other spiritual practices profoundly shifts your energy. I have learned the power of this connection from two teachers: Reverend Stretton Smith's writings for Unity classes and from a fellow coach and gifted meditation teacher, Linda Kolker, who uses heart meditation for students. It helps them connect more deeply with their feelings and with the Divine.

Smith writes about how the center of consciousness is in the heart. He urges us to feel into our hearts. Smith shares that he had been struggling to connect with God through his mind. At one point, in frustration, he asked, "Oh, God, help me love you." The next day he heard: "Put your mind in your heart and love God." As he transferred his attention to his heart, he felt a profound shift and felt grace pouring through him.

After reading this testimonial from Smith, I tried feeling into my heart space while praying and was astounded at how powerful the feeling was. One of the first times I did this was when my car was about to break down going over a mountain while seventy-five managers waited for me to arrive and run a team-building meeting. I was immediately filled with peace and calm and my car stopped clanking.

We are given wise guidance from a wealth of sources about the power of our hearts. In the Old Testament's book of Jeremiah is the directive "I will put my laws into their minds, and write them on their hearts."

An Islamic mystic said, "When the love of God arises in your heart, without doubt, God also feels love for thee."

Some cultures see the wisdom of the heart being part of the knowingness of the mind. In Chinese, the words for heart and mind are the same: *Hsin.*

The nineteenth-century Russian Orthodox mystic St. Theophane the Recluse devoted his spiritual practice to the phrase: *"Stand before God with your mind in your heart and love him."*

And these words which I command you [this day] shall be [upon the] heart.

—Deuteronomy 6:6

Is God upon our hearts, waiting for them to open?

Our hearts are more connected to our souls than our minds. Our language is filled with words that testify to this: heartfelt, heartbroken, heartsick, and a full heart. I feel my feelings strongest in my heart. When my child died, I felt a piercing of my heart. When I pray, I feel an expanding of my heart. When I am blissful, I feel lightness in my heart. Sometimes when I am visualizing something I want, I feel heat in my heart.

ALLOW GOD'S LOVE TO FLOW

Visualize God's love as a river flowing. Picture your heart as a dam holding back the river until small cracks start to form in its walls. Feel God's love start to flow through the openings until it washes over the wall, completely breaking through. Invite that energy into you. You are a channel of God's love. You are beautiful, powerful, and magnificent.

The Practice of Samyama

The guided heart meditation Samyama focuses on the heart center to feel God. The practice of Samyama is one way to meet what is, in order to experience the grace that is inherent in all situations, even the worst, most heartbreaking ones. Every experience, no matter how awful, can open to grace, to love, to peace, if we are willing to feel *what is*.

My fellow coach, Linda Kolker, has guided me in this heart meditation. She guides people as they sink deeply into their heart space. As feelings came up for me, instead of allowing me to go back into my head to analyze them, she urged me to feel underneath the thought, to feel what I wanted to express.

While working with this meditation, I felt great poignancy. I wept with recognition of what I had in my heart and that I was reconnecting with my Divine self. My tears were from sorrow and regret that it had taken me so long to return, and gratitude, joy, and bliss at knowing the depths my heart contained.

OPEN YOUR HEART

Feel into your heart space. Really allow yourself to sink into the depths of your heart. Experience its warmth. Feel your heart space expand and deepen. When a thought or feeling arises, don't analyze it. Just feel it—fully feel it without pushing it away.

Breathe into the beauty of your heart space. Visualize yourself being held by your heart as if a small child in a womb. Really enjoy that sense of being held. Send yourself love.

Say Yes with Your Heart

I urge you to put your mind in your heart. Trust what is happening. Say yes. Our hearts are so juicy. So spacious, so big. When I listen to God, this is what I hear:

Go where your heart calls you. That is the crux of feeling. Opening your heart to me. Feeling me fill it. Finding me always there when you can sink into me.

Your heart's desire is really a call for me. Receiving is the key. I am always here. One must receive me in. Open your arms to me. Open your heart to me. Open your mind to me. I rest in you.

CHAPTER 8

Partaking of Divine Communion

As I started this book, I was confident that I could write about having Divine communion with God. After all, I have experienced many conversations with God.

I reinforced these experiences during a workshop when A Course in Miracles teacher, Jon Mundy, asked if any of us believed we had had a mystical experience in our life. I shared that I have mystical experiences every day.

And I do. I feel the bliss of God moving through me. I feel God talking to me all the time, usually through signs: items people send to me, a song on the radio, a book I feel drawn to pick up, metaphors in my life, or tarot cards. I hear God guide me as I work with my coaching clients, knowing just the right questions to ask and insight to give them. I hear God through a wise voice in my head, through my body's wisdom, through my feelings, and through daily meditation. I ask God questions, pray to God, thank God, and cocreate my life with God.

But later I realized I had never sat down like Neale Donald Walsch has and actually had a two-way dialogue with God.

Yes, I understood God's language and was always listening for God's signs to me. Yes, I had called out in crisis and heard an answer, but never had I sat down while calm and happy and expected a back-and-forth conversation like you would have with a loved one.

When I came to that realization, what was most surprising was the "yikes" and the shiver of fear I felt. After all, I WANT to partake of Divine communion.

So I tried. And guess Who came through?! You know it. GOD.

I have felt God talk to me many times, but as much as I loved the *Conversations with God* books, I never thought about sitting down with a notepad or at my computer with my eyes closed and typing what I hear come through.

I had a disconnect between my belief that we can all partake of Divine communion and actually doing it. Here I was preaching that everybody can talk to God, and I was holding back because deep inside I felt it would be presumptuous, self-important—and scary. I was having trouble finding the courage to do it. I worried people would think that I was mentally ill.

Or maybe God would not talk to me. When I examined my feelings, I realized I had a lot of resistance to having an active conversation rather then being a passive receiver.

Talking the Talk, Walking the Walk

My resistance reminded me of when I taught persuasion at the University of Virginia. One of the strongest methods to persuade people is to show them they have a disconnect between their values and their beliefs. Recognizing this disconnect is called cognitive dissonance, and it is when people finally see that one value or belief they hold contradicts another of their values or beliefs.

It can also occur when someone's actions are not matching his or her values. When people come to see the contradiction between the two, they are forced to consider changing. They feel the dissonance and it makes them uncomfortable. They clearly see that they may be talking the talk but are not walking the walk.

I had a massive heart-thumping case of cognitive dissonance regarding my fervent belief that all of us should learn how to have conversations with God and being scared silly to try a two-way conversation.

I believe that we are all worthy to have a conversation with God—and that God is waiting for us to do so. Yet somewhere in my belief system lurked a sense of not being worthy enough and that if I did have a conversation with God, then I was trying to be bigger than I should be, even though I truly believe we are bigger, wiser, and more powerful than we give ourselves credit for. I tell my clients that all the time!

As I started to contemplate having a two-way conversation, all those faces of God that I had created faded away. A gentle Mother/Father God was nowhere to be found. A sense of God being so spacious, loving, and part of me disappeared in the face of fear. Instead, I was once again thinking of God as "the Big Guy" or "the

Man." It was like I had reverted to old patterns of what I had been taught about God in childhood, and it was holding me back from connecting. I was filled with fear, doubt, and self-criticism. I was back to feeling unworthy.

My inner critic had a field day. I heard it whisper to me: "It is one thing to encourage people to talk to God; it is another to have the presumption to think God will have a two-way dialogue with you. People will think you are nuts. People will think you are blasphemous. Who gives you the authority to talk for God? *Why would God talk to YOU?*"

Neale Donald Walsch had these same concerns during his conversations with God. He worried that he was being blasphemous and that he was not a worthy messenger. And some who read his book concluded that about him. But thousands more were inspired and touched by his words.

I started to feel great empathy for Walsch's predicament. Once I did begin, I couldn't slink away as if my conversations with God did not exist. To be in integrity, I needed to share how it went. That meant not only facing my resistance, but also experiencing resistance from others.

Why Would God Talk to Me?

Our resistance can start as soon as something happens in childhood that makes us feel separate from our divinity. As children, we start out knowing that God talks to us. When I ask my children if God talks to them, they answer, "Of course." Yet when something breaks this confidence, we start to doubt our worthiness.

I shared this with a book festival audience recently. I told the audience that as much as I encouraged others to connect to God, I ended up facing the question "Why would God want to talk to me?" Afterward someone came up and suggested I write a children's book about the subject so that children did not carry these fears into adulthood.

I started to sense what I was up against when my dad was helping me edit this book. My father, who is incredibly supportive of me, is a professor who has edited and authored twelve books and I value his opinion greatly. While writing a chapter, I included a quote from *Conversations with God* and attributed it to God. My dad took issue with that attribution and argued that God did not say that. When I asked how he knew, his response was that it wasn't in the Bible and this was Walsch writing and not God.

I realized in that moment what a struggle it is for so many of us to believe that God even talks to us. We think of our God as antiquated and only uttering guidance in a document thousands of years old, instead of a living, vibrant God who interacts with us now.

This same debate goes on in every spiritual tradition. Rumi notes this:

> **It is said that after Muhammad and the prophets, revelation does not descend upon anyone else. Why not? In fact it does, but then it is not called "revelation." It is what the Prophet referred to when he said, "The believer sees with the Light of God." When the believer looks with God's Light, he sees all things: the first and the last, the present and the absent. For how can anything be hidden from God's Light? And if something is hidden, then it is not the Light of God. Therefore the meaning of revelation exists, even if it is not called revelation.**

Fear of Change

So if revelation can come to the believer, why is it that there is so much resistance? Most of us are not going to publish our conversations with God or even tell our closest loved ones. The only ones who need to know are God and you. Yet even in that confined universe of two, we still have to face our greatest fear: that talking to God will change our lives.

Caroline Myss crystallizes this fear:

> **Deep in our cell tissue, we know that a mystical experience of the divine melts away doubts. We want it, we fear it, we know that it will empower our souls to reorganize our lives and priorities. We know instinctively that the more mystically we see the world, the more we will be inspired to take action. So, to keep this mystical consciousness at bay, to keep the status quo, we deliberately nurture untrue doubts in ourselves and in God.**

—*Entering the Castle*, page 33

Partaking of Divine communion definitely changes our lives. When we can summon up the courage and strength to have this conversation, we start building up our soul's muscle to heed the guidance that comes from it.

Right after my first non-crisis, extended, two-way conversation with God, I walked into my publicist's office and said timidly, "I decided if I'm writing a book about having a conversation with God, I needed to try it, so I did. And guess who answered?"

My publicist, who is spiritual, reacted the same way I had. She swallowed hard and said, "Oooh, that is scary."

Yes, it is. I felt myself gulp when she said that. All that I write about—from the mystics throughout time who doubted their messages but soldiered on with their relationship with God to believing you are worthy to speak to God—was staring me in the face. All that I represented rested on facing my fear.

Consider what challenges you face as you embark upon this new relationship with God. It takes courage and strength to approach God directly and expect an answer. In the past, people have had spiritual directors to guide them on this path. Spiritual directors help build up the soul's muscle slowly so people are not overwhelmed by the intensity of Divine union. Myss's book *Entering the Castle* provides a blueprint for this quest. In it she gives step-by-step guidance.

Build the stamina of your soul: It's a necessity.

—Caroline Myss, *Entering the Castle*, page 61

FEAR FACTOR

Ask yourself this question ten times and write down the answer that first comes to you each time: What holds you back from having a two-way conversation with God? Now consider these questions: What fears are you still holding onto about talking directly to God and expecting an answer? What are old messages that may still be getting in the way?

Step Slowly but Surely

Often, spiritual practices were passed down within a specific lineage and were only shared when the elders felt an individual was ready to receive the next step. Between the opening up of the Catholic Church through Vatican II and the surge of Eastern practices that entered the United States in the 1960s and 1970s, what had once been secret mystical practices became available. The exodus of Buddhist lamas from Tibet to the West provided access to ways that only monks and nuns had learned before.

So it makes sense that we approach a two-way conversation with God with courage and strength and the understanding that we need to take small steps to build the muscle of the soul. It is not required that you find a spiritual director, or that you dedicate yourself to spiritual exercises that require extreme discipline. What is necessary is to move slowly, but without doubt, as you approach God.

Remember, we are spiritual warriors and part of our training is to develop practices that support our path and commit to these practices as a discipline. We don't want a one-time flash-in-the-pan intense experience. Rather we want to build a daily relationship with God through discipline and cultivated silence, so we can listen to Her.

The sun makes the day bright, the moon makes the night beautiful, discipline adds to the dignity of a warrior; so quiet meditation distinguishes the seeker for Enlightenment.

—*The Teaching of Buddha,* page 376

Stretching toward God

My spiritual teacher always cautions: Take care of yourself. As a coach I say this: Stretch past your fears and resistance into a new place beyond your comfort zone, but do not push yourself too far.

I often use the comparison of a rubber band to help people see what stretching requires of us. To hold a rubber band between two fingers, we must create some tension and stretch so it doesn't just hang there. Yet we must not stretch it too tightly or it will break. We want to create just the right amount of tension.

When we move to new places and experience new growth, we often encounter a dip as if we no longer move ahead but instead lose ground. Right before the growth, we feel like we have gone backward. Like a child with a growth spurt, we trip over our larger feet until we get used to them. So, as I prepared to have my two-way conversation with God, I tumbled into a dip. I discovered that as much as I preached about God being love, I had gone into fear.

I am still working through it. In fact, it has become quite a joke between God and me. (Yes, God does have a great sense of humor.)

> ## STRETCHING TOWARD GOD
> What is a way you can stretch toward God? What could you do that will push you past your comfort zone?

My Conversation with God

So I finally had direct interactive Divine communion with God. I sat at my computer, with my eyes closed, and asked God to come to me. It was quiet for a long time. Then I heard a faint answer that I rejected at first. But I started to record it and when I listened closely it grew stronger.

My first conversation went like this:

How do I help people recognize God?

I am all. I am nothing. I am more than you will ever be able to get your arms around.

Um . . . am I really hearing this? I doubt I am having this experience.

It is something not to be doubted. You may trust it. I Am the great I Am.

How can I guide people to you?

It is necessary to start at the beginning. Invite people to have the view of me the way they want. Trust their wisdom, their perspective, their adulthood, their maturity to create me so they can connect with me.

What else should I tell them?

I am waiting. I am waiting right here patiently. Waiting for you—all of you. Waiting for your sight to be clear enough, your hearing to be strong enough, your heart to be open enough. I am right here. Can't you feel me? I am here. I am the deepest deep, the widest wide, the fullest full. Sink into me. Feel your heart rejoin mine. Rest in me. Your weary spirit cannot be renewed without me; no trouble not solved, no joy not celebrated!

It took me a while to get the courage up to have another conversation. My next conversation went like this:

Okay, God, I'm going to try talking to you again. Hi.
Hi back.

I love you.
I know you love me. My love is your love, your love is my love—it is always circulating.

I always feel so weepy when I feel you. I feel the tears welling up in my eyes right now.
It is your heart longing to move past the separation. To jump over the gully you've dug. Your heart is leaping out of your chest toward me. You need not leap over—you just need to ask me to come. I am here. I'm all around you. Feel me, and trust that you feel me.

(I was still fearful. God, who senses everything, called me on it.)
You are still afraid to talk to me, aren't you? That shudder! All this time we have spent together and you are still afraid of me. My darling, I'm here for you. You are like the starstruck teenager afraid to approach someone she admires from afar. It is like you are thrilled to write me love letters from a distance, but you don't want a direct two-way conversation. What is it that you fear? I'm not going to make you be a nun! I know you love me. I love you. What is it you are afraid of?

I don't know. I feel my eyes filling full of tears. I feel such longing to be with you and yet I shy away from it.
It has to do with not feeling worthy enough. Oh, I know, you really believe you have crossed that block to self-love. You feel like you know you are worthy, worthy enough to be with me.

Yet fear holds you back. Fear of not being enough. Fear of being swallowed up or controlled by me. Fear I will be like a parent. Fear I will ask you to do what you most don't want to do. You still have fear and resistance to calling on me directly. Look at that. It can help your readers. You are still afraid of what I might ask you to do. You are still afraid that I will ask you to stretch beyond where you want to go or do something unpleasant. Banish that thought, my child. There is no room for fear when you feel my love. Depend on the love to give you the courage to continue. What are you writing about? Are you not writing about trusting in this relationship? Who taught you not to trust in me? You are being defined by your fear.

You got me there. Using my own words against me.

Ah well, I inspired them.

(I laugh.)

Now you are amused. That is better.

Accepting That God Is There

After several conversations, I still doubted that God's voice came to me. I struggled over whether I was imagining it. Yet deep inside my heart I felt a peace I had never known. I felt a deep knowing—a knowing that God was indeed talking to me.

Yet my mind kept asking me if God was there.

God, are you there?

Of course I am here, Michelle. Is this not what you are writing about? That I am always here, that I am all around and inside of you. You have quite a sense of humor asking if I'm here.

Okay, okay, I get it. I still doubt myself sometimes.

It is natural; everyone does. The mystics just do it less. They start honoring that voice.

What do I need to tell people?

You need to tell people that I don't care how they see me. That I just want to love them, and for me to fully love them they need to be able to receive it.

Receiving is the key. Many of you spend all your energy on creating ,but if you can't receive what you have asked for, then you are in big trouble. You know this. How many times have you attached PS's to a request you make that sabotages what you ask for? It is like saying to the Universe, "Yes, I want this, but PS, not yet."

I like your way of talking about keeping your energy clean, and not having static in your field. Of course, it is harder to practice this, n'est-ce pas?

I smile.

I like the flicker of a smile that just crossed your face.

Accepting That God Is Everywhere

The next time I had my conversation I felt lighter about my fear.

All right God, I am waiting with fear and apprehension (laughing).

Oh, Michelle, I am like the sun, here to warm you, not to frighten you.

What do I need to write about feeling?

Tell them to trust their feelings. They are the gateway to me. If they trust their feelings, they trust that they can feel me. When the head is in the way of the heart, then there is trouble.

Why do I feel called to write this book?

When your child died, you called on me. Yes, I feel your pain as we bring this up. Yet you did not blame me. You used it to connect with me more. To reach out to me. Don't you remember that after you delivered her, after they rushed her out of the room to resuscitate her and returned to tell you she died, as you lay on the table bleeding, you asked for a chaplain?

You asked for someone who could help remind me of you, because you did not forget me. You knew, even as your child died, that I had not forgotten you.

And then you learned how to call on me and ask for what you wanted. And surrender to me how I would bring it into your life.

I start to cry.

You are touched. You are moved. Yes, that is part of your beauty. Beauty. Life is full of beauty. Beauty is a way to feel me. Love is a way to feel me. Gratitude is a way to feel me. Appreciation is a way to feel me. Call on me. Ask for me.

How do I teach others to feel you?

When they feel love, they feel me. Talk to them about feeling their body, and the space around their body. Teach them to allow joy to arise, allow love to arise. Allow love of who they are to arise. That is part of surrender. Their heart's desire is really a call for me.

What do I talk about in terms of bringing up feelings for you?

The first step is willingness. Even if they are afraid, it is willingness—a willingness not to shut down the joy, the love, the warmth in their body, their highest selves; a willingness to open themselves to me. Have them feel me there in their heart, in their body, in the room with them, or if that is too much of a step, have them feel me coming. Remind them that their feelings are the key to their lives. Feel your feelings. And yet don't let emotions rule you. Go out into nature to reconnect with me. Feel me in the trunk of the tree, the call of a birdsong, the sweetness of the scent of grass, the vibrancy of a blossom. You know you have found me when you feel recognition. I am in you. Have you ever made a new friendship that felt like you had known the person for a long time? You have known me for a long time. You just forgot.

I am all. I am nothing. I am more than you will ever be able to get your arms around. Yes, it's something not to be doubted. I am the great I Am. Invite people to me. Have a birthday party for me. Celebrate my I Am–ness the way you would celebrate a birthday.

Believing That God Can Speak to You

I decided to ask for guidance about how to help others move past the block of believing God cannot speak to them. After all, if I felt it come up so strongly, surely others would experience this.

Why is it that we believe that God can come to other people but not us? Repeatedly people have believed others' experiences over their own.

You feel Me, yet know few would believe. The biggest challenge with feeling is really believing and honoring your belief. The mystics continuously had to get encouragement from others, often superiors, to write down their experiences. They too felt like they faltered and thought perhaps they were making it up. Neale Donald Walsch questioned himself.

How do I guide people in having a conversation with you?

Talk about the fear. How many people go into the dark night of the soul? That is not necessary to reach me, but it is a way to me. Some people would never come to me without it. But if their path is through love, and that means self-love, and they can let of attachment, the way is easier.

First one must overcome the resistance that comes up about approaching me, then one must overcome the "am I crazy?"— something all the mystics had to do, although those grounded in spiritual traditions that believed these things did not have to do this as much. They had support. Yet almost everyone has doubted they hear me. It is their voice of fear that causes them to reject the voice of love. My voice is of love. How could one not want to come toward love? Why would someone move to fear?

I am anxious.

Stay steady, girl. You have made this journey. You have much to tell. You are afraid of losing yourself. Yet, darling, you find yourself in me. It is not an abyss; it is a vast expansiveness you are entering. You will not fall.

People cling to what they know out of fear. Yet when you let go, like the child not wanting to let go of the side of the pool, or standing on a high dive and finally jumping, you feel exhilaration. Have not the best things come out of your biggest risks?

Yes. Yes, they have!

Take courage. We have much work to do. We are waking up the world or at least those who are slumbering lightly. You are one of many who have been chosen at this time to do this. The world is opening. It is becoming more conscious. I'm here. How did you start to have a conversation with me? You took it in stages. Got your toes wet first. You went from small signs to bigger, bolder requests. Share this. Talk about stages. Let people ease into relationship with me. Then they too will help me wake up the world.

EASING INTO THE CONVERSATION

Try a few of these steps. When you feel ready for your conversation with God (well, ready the way one is about jumping off the high dive—my experience proved we are rarely entirely ready), center yourself and ask for God to come through. Then wait in silence. You may wait a long time. You may hear a faint voice or think your imagination is playing tricks on you. But if you wait, and start trusting the process, God will come through to you.

God advises us to ease into the conversation and to approach Her in stages. What stages have you taken to approach God? Do you have a prayer practice? Are you meditating? Have you written a letter from God to yourself?

Claiming Your Right to Partake of Divine Communion

This book has urged you to claim your Divine inheritance. Each of us found OUR God, the God we want, and worked to dissolve resistance by letting go of all those images that don't serve us.

We allowed ourselves to feel God and let God embrace us through our feelings.

Now we have to receive that we *can* have a direct conversation. Realize that messages really do come, that God does talk to us, and that the God, in our image, is someone we are safe with. We are not talking to an angry, vengeful God. We are talking to someone who really wants to listen. And really wants to answer.

Stay steady and keep returning to God. Not every conversation is going to be a peak experience. A voice may not always come. Sometimes God will speak to you through other channels. Sometimes you will doubt yourself. Sometimes you will waver. Sometimes you will lose your way. Sometimes you will lose your focus. Sometimes you will cave to the fear.

Come, come, whoever you are. Wonderer, worshipper, lover of leaving. It doesn't matter. Ours is not a caravan of despair. Come, even if you have broken your vow a thousand times. Come, yet again, come, come.

—Rumi

Come back yet again. Always come again.

CLAIMING YOUR RIGHT

Claim your right to have a two-way conversation with God. Come up with ten answers to this question: What is right about having a two-way conversation with God?

Start trusting the process, God will come through to you.

CHAPTER 9

Receiving God's Guidance

I sat on the large rock where I meditate at the cabin overlooking the twin mountain creeks and I gave thanks for the many gifts in my life. I gave thanks for having a solid rock to ground me, two streams to sing to me, and a place to go for silence.

I asked God for help in mastering the Law of Attraction. I asked how to guide people. I sat for a long time in silence. Then I heard a voice.

One day, on the rock at the twin streams, while meditating and listening in silence, this is what I heard:

I love you. Each one of you already holds the secret of creation, for it comes from self-remembering. You just need to honor yourself, for I am in you.

Stretch into your Highest Self. When you know your Highest Self, then you know that we are all one and what you ask for benefits all because it will cause your light to shine.

Respond to the call of your soul and my light will shine on you and you will reflect it outward. Each of you will be a light to others.

I love all my children. I want my children to cocreate their lives with me. I give gifts freely to those who ask. I expect my children to ask. Each of you needs to learn to ask, and allow in what you want.

Ask me for guidance as to whether what you ask for is in alignment with your soul. You can ask me how to cocreate your life.

I am waiting for each of you.

Learn to receive yourself and love yourself **because this is your sacred duty.**

Then you need to surrender—for in surrendering, my work can be done. Once you ask, you must let go of the outcome, for it is time to receive. This means the striving goes away; the controlling goes away. By surrendering after asking, you lessen your resistance to it coming to you.

A Direct Channel

As I sat there, listening, I felt like a direct channel had opened up.

Is there more?

First ask for yourself. As you grow in love and are able to receive my gifts, then you ask for others. Come to me for healing, but then start to heal others and you will fully heal. Ask for things that make the world a better place. Be a model, a gift in this world, so that others may gently grow. Reach for love—experiences, things, and people who embody love.

Sometimes people do not know how to reach toward love. Fear keeps people stuck, trapped. If a car was going to run over your child, you would throw yourself in front of it. If a man was going to attack your family, you would fight him.

You do this because of the love you feel for others. Are you not worthy of this love also? Why do you not marshal this energy for yourself? Why do you not fight for yourself?

Fight for yourself in the choices you make about where you put your focus. It means seeing what good can come into your life, and not giving power to the negative things. Fight for a life lived in the light.

Every minute of every day make a decision to reach toward love. Be present to your feelings, honor them, and make the next choice in that minute to love yourself. That means making choices that are loving to you and others. Live centered in your soul. Do not let the external dictate who you are.

Live inside out, not outside in. *You set your vibration. You choose how to respond to external things. Yes, truly feel your feelings but then choose another way to look at them.*

Never forget who you are. In remembering yourself, you remember me.

Receiving YOUR Guidance from God

We all can receive direct guidance. Ask God directly about how you can master the Law of Attraction. Sit with a pad and paper or a computer and write down what comes to you. It is an experience that will redefine you.

We can "know" things intellectually, but to really know spiritual concepts, they must sink into us until they transform us. They must become so much a part of our belief system that we start to feel and the feeling reawakens our soul.

For example, there is a difference in reading lots of books about how we are all one and having a mystical experience of truly feeling one. Experiencing being one with the floor, the table, the grass, the flowers, the ant crawling on your leg is mind blowing. It is like a spiritual acid trip when you feel your body melt into everything else. Bliss arises. Suddenly, there is no separation.

The same goes for experiencing the Law of Attraction through God. No longer is the focus on just "getting." Instead, a God who wants us to live in joy and cocreate our highest good bathes us in love.

The Law of Attraction is the Law of Love. When used correctly, it is one of the strongest indicators of God's love for us. By learning how to master it, we expand ourselves and raise up those around us just by our positive energy and high vibrations.

God wants to teach us how to use this law. We must merely ask Him.

Rock-a My Soul

I love the African American hymn "Rock-a my soul."

Rock-a my soul in the bosom of Abraham,
Oh, rock-a my soul.

So high you can't get over it,
so low you can't get under it,
so wide you can't get around it,
Oh, rock-a my soul.

Now there is one expanded soul! A soul that lives from the inside out, a soul that does not live conditionally on what is out there but emanates a vibration from inside.

When I think about the messages I received on the rock, I started calling them the **"Rock-a my soul" Seven Steps for the Law of Attraction.** Here are the seven steps:

1. Ask and, in asking, move toward love.
2. Live centered in your soul.
3. Remember who you are and stretch into your Highest Self.
4. Reach for love.
5. Surrender the outcome to God.
6. Live inside out, not outside in.
7. Receive.

Step by Step

In dividing out this wisdom systematically, some key concepts emerge:

1. Ask and, in asking, move toward love.

Ask and, in asking, you move toward self-love, for you are saying "I am worthy" to ask. It is a declaration that "I am a precious child of God and it is my birthright to ask."

[W]e don't ask God for too much, in fact we ask God for too little. . . . all we have to do is ask for His help. The help might not come in the form we expected . . . but it will come, and we will recognize it by how we feel.

—Marianne Williamson, *A Return to Love,* page 84

Ask and you shall receive is more than just about getting what you want. It is the first direction to head in as you embark on creating your new life. Ask God for guidance. Ask how to use the Law of Attraction so that you can use it masterfully.

Set your compass to true north: *your* God. You will sense you are on the right path and will feel God's hand guiding you in your travels. Be alert for signs that you are rowing your boat in the wrong direction. God may send you subtle hints. Perhaps you just need to alter your course a little bit or change how you approach rough waters.

I want what you want.

—Neale Donald Walsch,
Conversations with God, Book 1, page 49

ASK

Stop right now and ask God if you are moving in the right direction. What first comes to your mind? What do you hear? How does your body feel? Do this often and see what different reactions come up, depending on the situation.

2. Live centered in your soul.

Your inner core is your soul. Stay centered and in touch with your soul's desires. Often we delude ourselves by thinking we can fill ourselves up with material possessions. Material possessions can bring joy and contentment if they are truly desired but they cannot fill the holes we have in our souls. We have to do this by identifying these holes through self-discovery and asking God to make us whole again.

You must make sure what you are asking for is in alignment with your soul's highest purpose. You can do this by asking for guidance and signs that you are going in the right direction. **You start to BE what you really want.** Material possessions and success are available, but even greater riches come: knowing who you are and knowing God.

Know yourself and heed your soul's call. Remember that God is always in the equation. Jesus said, "Nothing I do, I can do without my father."

LIVE CENTERED IN YOUR SOUL

What does living centered in your soul mean to you? Come up with a definition to guide you.

3. Remember who you are and stretch into your Highest Self.

When you think of yourself as powerless and a victim, you have forgotten yourself. Remember yourself as the powerful, magnificent being that you are. You are a piece of God and when you bond yourself with God, your power is infinite.

Your soul already knows Who You Really Are. It is waiting for the rest of you to catch up. Stretch into your Highest Self. You will know you are there by the way you feel. Neale Donald Walsch tells us that God says that in some moments we already know that we are the deepest wisdom and the highest truth, the greatest peace and the grandest love.

REMEMBER YOUR HIGHEST SELF

Think about times when it felt like you were coming from your Highest Self. How did you act? How did you feel?

4. Reach for love.

In every choice, in every experience, and in every relationship, reach for love.

Retrain yourself. Stay in your heart space. Make choices that are loving and kind. Do not engage in self-abuse and self-loathing, whether from situations in which you place yourself or the way your mind chatters and your inner critic treats you. This is as much about your internal life as your external life.

Reach for situations that are loving and supportive. Be aware of how people and environments impact your sense of peace and feelings of joy. I used to think I wasn't "spiritual" enough if I couldn't hold my center in my marriage or during a chaotic political campaign. What I didn't realize was that I needed to remove myself from situations that were self-abusive, as they wore me down and lowered my vibrations. I could not regain my equilibrium in the midst of them.

Yes, my soul's muscle eventually strengthened enough so that I could enter a situation with chaos and hold my center. First, I needed to learn how to do so in a loving, nurturing environment.

Give yourself a respite so that you can come to your center again. Quiet down your inner chatter. Look around, see the beauty in your life, and reside in gratitude and appreciation.

Remember, as you grow in love, you heal others. You were not sent here to fix a broken world, but through actions and energy, you can help heal it. Do not take this on as a heavy task but instead as a joyful assignment to bring light to the world. Be an uplifter, a bringer of light, a healer to those in your life. You cannot fix them through the Law of Attraction or God's love. They must take this on for themselves.

What you can do is ask that your love bring them healing by being in their lives and modeling love, joy, and power. Choosing to live the life that you want—a life filled with joy, power, passion, and meaning—is choosing love.

What we are charged with is choosing love in each moment. This is as simple as reframing a negative experience so that you do not stay stuck in it. Doing so takes courage. It means breaking old patterns. When you are a victim, you don't have to take responsibility for your life. You can stay stuck in fear.

When you choose love, you choose power—a spiritual power that allows you to know you are never alone. You always have God to turn to for guidance.

But the Counselor, the Holy Spirit, whom the Father will send in my name, will teach you all things and will remind you of everything I have said to you. Peace I leave with you; my peace I give you. I do not give to you as the world gives. Do not let your hearts be troubled and do not be afraid.

—John 14:26–27

REACH FOR LOVE

Think about a negative situation that recently occurred. How could you have reached for love? What would that have looked like for you to have reached for love? What are ways you can reach for love each day?

5. Surrender the outcome to God.

Allow God to do Her work. When you demonstrate your faith in God and let go, this generates the place of least resistance. Stay in faith with it. Once you ask for something, don't attach to the outcome. Let go and trust that it will come to you. Esther and Jerry Hicks, through the channeled teachings of Abraham, talk about the great manager in the sky who attends to all the details. They urge us not to create more resistance to receiving what we want by worrying that the manager won't get it right.

God is this manager. Many times I have worried that what I want is not coming, only for it to show up in ways far grander than I imagined. My clients share stories of how the perfect soul mate, job, house, or vacation appeared and at first they almost rejected the gift because it wasn't exactly what they expected.

ALLOW GOD TO DO HER WORK

Is there something you are worrying about? Have you set an intention and wonder if you are doing the right things to make it manifest in your life?

Retrain these thought patterns by reminding yourself that God needs you to move out of the way so She can do Her work.

6. Live inside out, not outside in.

Just as you must learn to love unconditionally, you must learn to live without conditions. Your joy and happiness is not dependent on others to make it so. You are responsible for your life. You must learn your inner landscape and stay steadily on your journey. Engage in self-discovery.

Do not live in this world conditionally, dependent on what happens to you to determine how and who you are. Sometimes this means removing yourself from a situation to find peace and gain equilibrium. Often it means reframing a situation and working to attract in new positive experiences.

Let your life be lived from inside, instead of letting the external world control your inner world.

LIVE INSIDE OUT

Think of something stressful. Think about the core of your being and your Highest Self. How can you react in this situation by living from the inside out, instead of living from the outside in? What would your Highest Self do?

7. Receive.

Give yourself permission to receive. Know that you are worth it. Don't be the child who stares longingly at a piece of cake that is offered but is too shy to accept it. Say yes.

You deserve it. You are worthy. Receiving is a sign of being a spiritual follower. To receive and respond to gifts is generous and loving.

OPEN YOUR ARMS WIDE

As you say your wants aloud, preface them with the words "I receive."

A Big "Aha"

. . . Oh God who gives the grace of vision! The bird of vision is flying towards You with the wings of desire.

—Rumi, Mystic Odes 833

That day on the rock, I began to understand how the Law of Attraction worked within the sphere of God and the Universe. The more aligned we are with our Highest Self and the more we move to love, the higher our vibration becomes. With an expanded soul, we are more successful at creating the life we want.

PERMISSION TO RECEIVE

State a want that you have starting with "I receive with gratitude. . . ." Make sure you phrase it in the present tense as if it is already here.

Simple but Not Always Easy

The "Rock-a my soul" seven steps are simple but not always easy to apply. All the teachings on the Law of Attraction share similar themes: We are more powerful than we know, we must simply ask and it is given, and our thoughts and feelings create our reality. Getting to mastery on these is a different story.

Moving these concepts from intellectual ideas into a way of living requires passion and perseverance. It is a lifetime of work and all training is on-the-job. Be easy with yourself and don't expect to get all the nuances the first time around.

And if you think you have them down pat, it's a good sign that you don't. Almost all people who consciously use the Law of Attraction have areas in their lives they have not mastered. If you had nothing left to learn, life would get boring.

Like many simple concepts, you can take your knowledge and mastery ever deeper.

Divine Communion Is a River That Quenches Your Thirst

Perhaps you started reading this book to discover more about the Law of Attraction. Maybe you were drawn to it because you wanted to deepen your relationship with God. Or you wanted to understand how the two are linked.

God and the Law of Attraction are inherently coupled. To become Who We Really Are we must learn to master the Law. We deepen our relationship with God when we turn to Her for guidance in mastering the Law.

When we see the Law of Attraction as one of God's gifts to us then it becomes part of our spiritual discipline to understand and consciously use it. We are like children who are grateful for the gifts given to us and learn how to take good care of them.

As we turn to God for guidance, we plunge ourselves into spiritual waters. We baptize ourselves not just in any water, but in a river of grace. Like the hymn that asks "Shall We Gather at the River?" we can choose to bring grace into our life's river. The river of life becomes not a place to fight the current but rather a source carrying us along, flowing with abundance.

> *Ere we reach the shining river,*
> *lay we every burden down;*
> *grace our spirits will deliver,*
> *and provide a robe and crown.*
> *Soon we'll reach the shining river,*
> *soon our pilgrimage will cease;*
> *soon our happy hearts will quiver*
> *with the melody of peace.*

CHAPTER 10

Receiving Gifts from God

Gifts come in all shapes and sizes. I have been graced with many. Sometimes my gifts arrived as a prayed-for child, other times a job that allowed me to provide a house for my children.

In order for my divorce to go through, I had either to sell my home or to refinance and buy out my husband's share. I felt strongly that I needed to keep the house during this time of transition so my children could have continuity with their home, their school, and their friends. We love our neighborhood; our home is two houses away from the neighborhood pool and located in a cul-de-sac where kids play.

The divorce lawyers drew up papers saying I needed to have proof that I could refinance the house by June.

I had yet to prove I could support my family with my coaching practice, and much of my energy had been sidetracked by the divorce. But each day I reminded myself that the right work would come to me.

I knew, deeply knew, I could refinance my house. I didn't know how, but I knew that circumstances would align so that I could. Yes, a nagging little voice popped up occasionally and told me I was a failure. And there were plenty of people around asking how in the world I was going to be able to do what I needed to do.

Then a city manager called me to talk about coaching his leadership team. It was the perfect fit for me after my years in politics, combining my coaching skills with an understanding of all the nuances of government.

I was given a one-year coaching contract to coach twenty-four managers, with payments spread out evenly each month. With this contract, signed right at the end of my June deadline, I was able to demonstrate to the bank that I could produce dependable income.

After my divorce, I didn't know how I was going to keep the house for my kids, but I knew that I was going to do it with God's help. God delivered an outcome in a way that I could not have imagined. The city coaching job was a wonderful experience. I was a good match and I learned so much about coaching a large team of people. My clients felt well served and, since they were directors of departments, some of them hired me to work in their offices. Because of the references I gathered and reputation I built, other local governments sought me out.

I could not have created a more perfect scenario. My children were able to stay in their home and my coaching career got a big boost. I matured into a more powerful coach. The contract helped me establish my reputation and it produced further work.

We Have to Let Gifts In

He will receive blessing from the Lord.
—Psalm 24:5

When God delivers, we must remember we are worthy of the gift and receive it even when we doubt our own ability. It would have been easy for me to self-sabotage this opportunity, considering my lack of confidence after being on the mommy-track for a few years and the emotional bruising while emerging from a divorce.

When an opportunity is laid at our feet, our work is to see it is a sign and have faith that we can handle it. We stretch and grow.

Rejecting Gifts

All of us have rejected gifts. I had a client who was in a miserable romantic relationship and an unfulfilling career. Every night she left a job that drained her to return to a home where she felt under attack.

She started to create a vision of a new life. Her dream was to live in a pastoral setting and have greater control of her life. Almost immediately, she inherited a farm where she could have her own home and relocate to a more positive job experience. She let this dream slip away because she was paralyzed by the fear of change and of being alone.

A male client called me, distraught because his girlfriend, a survivor of an abusive marriage, had decided she didn't deserve him. She broke up with him and told him to find another. He was heartbroken because he loved her and was grateful for her sweet temperament after being married to a critical ex-wife. He was ready to let her go without a fight because he feared that she had fabricated the story in order to reject him. With some encouragement, he went to her and told her how he felt and they reunited.

I have a dear friend who has a pattern of unhealthy relationships. An extremely successful and kind man was head over heels in love with her, yet she turned her interest to another who had the reputation of being unsavory and unkind. As she told the man who loved her that she didn't see their relationship going anywhere, he shed tears of grief for himself and concern for her.

Then one day as she was driving, she had an epiphany. She realized she felt unworthy of a good man who loved her and that is why she had refused to accept his love.

She called him immediately to share this insight, went right over to his home, and never left. Now they are married. By pulling back to recognize her patterns, she caught herself rejecting the kind of man she most wanted.

How many gifts have you not let in because you felt you were not ready, not qualified, or not worthy?

REFUSING GIFTS

Make a list of at least three opportunities you shied away from or rejected. List the reasons you used to reject the gift.

Remember *You* Are a Gift

When I listen to God, this is what I hear:

The greatest gift is you. **When you fully receive yourself, you receive me, for you can feel me in you.** *You recognize your magnificence. You realize you are enough. So also is there enough in our Universe.*

You are enough. *Whatever you are not yet, your Highest Self already is.* Your work is to catch up with what your Highest Self has already become. Framed in this way, therefore, you are merely bridging a gap—between who you think you are and your true Highest Self. Reminiscent of a child who can already taste the apple that he is reaching to pluck from the tree, you stretch toward who you really are. Like unharvested fruit, your magnificence sits within reach and your soul can already taste its sweetness.

RECEIVE YOURSELF AS A GIFT

Right now, say aloud, "I receive myself as a great gift from God. Thank you for myself and my life."

You Are Not Alone

When an opportunity comes your way, or a desire arises that you wish to pursue, always remember that not only do you have a Highest Self that creates success, but *you are not alone.*

I remember meeting with a minister who was describing, with great excitement, a speaking bureau she wanted to establish. Finally, I commented that the topic she wanted to bring experts in to speak about was *her* expertise. She was a strong, articulate, and graceful presence, and people always paused to listen when she spoke. I suggested that she do a series of talks instead.

Shaking her head, she told me she could never do that alone. I leaned forward, smiled, and reminded her that she was never alone. As tears welled up in her eyes, she said that, of all people, she should have remembered that, but her fear had gotten in the way.

A coach had the same fear about running workshops by herself. She always teamed up with someone, although often she had a greater passion for doing the workshop than her partner. During a coaching session, I urged her to consider running the workshops herself.

She replied she could never do a workshop by herself. When I suggested she was not by herself, that her Source was right there by her side to guide her, tears rolled down her cheeks and she said she had forgotten that it was not all up to her.

God Supports You

God does not give you opportunity only to allow you to fall flat on your face. When you walk in faith, you get what you need to succeed. I discovered this firsthand in writing this book on a short deadline. I prayed and asked for guidance and was told repeatedly "Supports will be given." Supports were given in the form of a cabin retreat to write in, babysitting arrangements for my children, coaching work to pay the bills, and time for writing.

During this period, I received a man into my life who I, at first, feared would be a distraction to my work. I soon learned he would be one of my greatest supports. Not only did he provide me with the cabin to write in, a private library to inspire me, and lots of encouragement, but he respected my boundaries and made no demands on my time, even reminding me that we had to be careful that he did not become a distraction. He is a great blessing in my life and my muse, someone who accepts me as I am and supports me in where I want to go.

I also manifested an experienced editor to guide me. When writing my first book proposal, for a different book, I realized one Sunday evening at nine o'clock that I needed an editor. I set the intention that I would find the right person.

Immediately, I recalled that a client who ran a marketing company had given me the name of an editor. I called the referral and quickly realized as we talked that I knew her. Valarie Massie Watersun, a smart and savvy author and editor whom I already admired, agreed to start editing that night so I could turn my book proposal in within a few days.

Although I expect miracles in my life, getting an experienced editor ready to work late on a Sunday night with a deadline looming is one for which I am particularly grateful! Valarie has edited both my books, helping give shape and clarity to my writing. Our working relationship, fueled by mutual respect, keeps the spark of my creativity lit. She has been a cheerleader keeping me inspired and committed.

In addition, my father's visits from his home in China where he teaches ended up timed at the beginning and end of the writing process, providing me with a knowledgeable additional editor and sounding board.

Everyday Miracles

What everyday miracles do you have in your life? Start counting your blessings. Look around every day and see what you have to be grateful for. As we learn to have discipline about gratitude, more gifts appear because we are receiving and giving thanks for what we have in our lives, thus signaling that we are ready to receive more.

Gratitude reframes how we see our lives. We start to see all the gifts we have, instead of focusing on what we don't yet possess. I was guided to this law while recovering from the biggest heartbreak in my life: the death of my first child.

When my little girl died, I felt like I wasn't going to make it through that first year. I had trouble getting out of bed in the morning and could barely function through the day. I knew my work was to feel the feelings and work through the grief because feelings that are buried just surface later in unhealthy ways. But I also needed to have a reason to live and that was hard to find.

I started keeping a gratitude journal and writing down five things I was grateful for each day. More than anything else I did that year, this practice of cultivating gratitude changed me. I was able to notice all the blessings in my life and celebrate them. I started to see the light in my life and it served as a lamp to lead me out of my darkness. Now I end each day with a moment to reflect on the gifts of my day and give thanks.

Many other people I know, by focusing on what they are grateful for, have had their lives changed. At a wedding, I met a young single mother who confessed to being dark and self-destructive at seventeen when she had her son. Her own mother had left when the daughter was still a teenager and she had lived with her father who was a drug dealer and an alcoholic.

She turned her life around by focusing on positive thoughts and keeping a gratitude journal. This brave young woman started collecting inspiring quotes about creating her life and living in positive energy. Her journal is so important to her that she keeps it in her purse at all times to help her stay upbeat and committed to her new outlook. Although her life is still not always easy, she is a happy, contented woman who lives in lightness and joy.

Enough

When we have gratitude, we realize all the riches we already have. If we are not able to see what we have or are not grateful for our blessings, we think that God doesn't give us what we need. We are like the ugly duckling that is really a swan but can't perceive his beauty because he can see only what the other ducks have.

Dr. Norman Vincent Peale, the author of many inspiring books including *The Power of Positive Thinking,* shares stories of sad individuals who told him that they had nothing in their lives. He challenged them by asking if their wife or husband had died, their home had burned, or their health was ruined. Each of them left, realizing their lives were filled with gifts, only to discover later that, as they changed their focus to gratitude, many more gifts arrived.

When we realize how much we have, we learn to view the world as abundant. We confront the old belief system that there is not enough. As we challenge this belief system, other self-sabotaging beliefs arise for us to look at and move beyond. The push to be aggressive and grab what we can before it's gone starts to relax. We realize that greed, avarice, stinginess, hoarding, and envy stem from that core belief.

We also learn we don't need to come from a place of lack or guilt, thinking that if we ask for what we want, there won't be enough to go around. The Universe does not operate on a chit system—I do for you if you do for me. Like the precious children we are, we are given our gifts because we are already loved. Miracles arrive not because we have done something to deserve them, but because we are worthy just by being God's children.

There really is enough. Until we can acknowledge this, it is hard to receive gifts. When we feel like there isn't enough to go around, we need to look at what we are doing to promote this thought.

ENOUGH

Make a list of the abundance already in your life. Come up with ten things and give thanks for them. They can be as simple as a beautiful day or laughing at something funny— or as important as your health or family.

Generosity Creates a Generous Universe

. . . he who sows sparingly will also reap sparingly, and he who sows bountifully will also reap bountifully.

—2 Corinthians 9:6

Sowing seeds bountifully means not only seeds of desire, but also seeds of generosity. In the Bible verse "Sow the wind, reap the whirlwind," we are reminded that what we put out in the world we get back. If we are giving, loving, and compassionate, that is what we get in return.

The ability to be authentically generous is linked with the belief that the world is abundant and what we give does come back to us to bless us further. Just as we enjoy receiving gifts, there is joy in giving gifts also. Our gifts can be as simple as taking the time to help someone or saying a kind word. A gift can be a smile or simple words of appreciation.

One of my favorite things to do when I am in a public setting is to stop and tell the cleaning staff that I appreciate what a good job they are doing. I get such a gift in return as I see these hard-working individuals light up with pride about their efforts. They always smile back at me.

To be generous means we believe we have enough to give back and faith that we will get what we need. This is not to say that we overreach and go beyond our resources to give, for we must always remember to act loving to ourselves. If we give beyond our capacity, we end up feeling depleted. When we give with a compulsive push or a martyr's energy, other people feel it and resent it. Through self-awareness, we can gauge when our giving is done with joy and without expectation.

Many prosperity teachers believe that tithing to a church or charity is the cornerstone of creating prosperity. They cite the Old Testament instruction to tithe to God. Although this was a hard concept for me to accept, I now give to my church, although I haven't reached the 10 percent goal.

Whether you choose to tithe your time, your talent, or your money to a cause or just to those you encounter every day, giving back lets God know that you see the abundance in your life.

I have a dear friend who has created fortunes out of practically nothing with this attitude. My friend owned a series of thriving businesses and chose to stop working in her forties. She owns millions of dollars of real estate in Washington, D.C. One of her principles is to give 10 percent to spiritual causes and charity because, she says, "If I show the Universe I feel abundant enough to share, the Universe gives me more."

A GENEROUS SPIRIT

What is a way you can cultivate generosity in yourself? Think about areas where you might not be generous—whether it is time, money, or kindness. Stretch into being more generous in this area. Take an action step this week toward that goal.

Ask as Prayer

Ernest Holmes, who founded the Religious Science/Science of the Mind movement, reminds us that just as we must plant a seed before we can reap a harvest, so we must believe before our prayers are answered. I might add that gratitude helps water the soil so that our desires can grow. Not only should we be grateful for what we already have, but we should also be grateful for what we are about to receive. Master manifesters understand the essential spiritual law about giving thanks for something before it has occurred. When we pray and have so much faith that we thank God before it happens, miracles do occur.

I was guided to this law after my child died. Trying hard did not make me pregnant, nor, when I finally got pregnant, did it save the life of my child. I did everything medically possible to save her life and could not.

I had to make peace with my inability to control everything through sheer willpower. I surrendered to Divine will with the knowledge that I couldn't force an outcome, but I could ask for one in prayer and thank God for its arrival before it even manifested. For the first time, instead of bulldozing over obstacles, I relaxed into asking with a calm assurance that my request would be granted.

After asking, I started lighting a candle with the word "abundance" on it. I started thanking God for sending me a baby girl through adoption and a baby boy through pregnancy. I did this every day and held the intention that this would occur.

The timing on this request was vital. At thirty-five, I was eager to create my family quickly, so I really wanted two babies. If I was too far along in my pregnancy, the adoption agency might deny my request. And after carrying a baby to term, only to have her die, the thought of going through another pregnancy without a baby in my arms was too painful. I felt guided to ask for a family created through adoption and pregnancy. Although I hadn't yet been exposed to the Law of Attraction, I felt confident that God would answer my prayer.

Ask and It Is Given

I asked and it was given. I found out I was pregnant and a month later got a referral for a baby girl from Russia. We traveled nine days later. Within six months time, I had two babies, a girl and a boy.

I was astounded. Exactly what I had asked for had been given to me. I knew I was living in grace.

What a profound life-changing way to learn the spiritual law of asking and receiving! Although my spiritual knowledge had deepened and moved beyond the Catholic belief system I had grown up with, nowhere had I read that the Universe worked like this.

Several years later, when I read *Conversations with God*, by Neale Donald Walsch, I was a believer, but the book helped clarify how to ask in prayer: Pray with gratitude as if you have already received your request.

In *Conversations with God*, we are taught to ask God carefully. If we say, "I want a new house," what we get is the "wanting" of the new house, not the new house.

> The word "I" is the key that starts the engine of creation. The words "I am" are extremely powerful. They are statements to the universe. Commands. Now, whatever follows the word "I" (which calls forth the Great I Am) tends to manifest in physical reality.
>
> Therefore "I" + "want money" must produce you wanting money. It can produce no other thing, because thoughts, words are creative. Actions are, too. And if you act in the way which says you want success and money, then your thoughts, words and actions are in accord and you are sure to have the experience of this wantingness.
>
> —Neale Donald Walsch, *Conversations with God, Book 1,* page 178

Conversations with God was the first book I read on manifesting, but I soon came to discover the wealth of writings on it, including *Excuse Me, Your Life Is Waiting,* by Lynn Grabhorn. Although many attribute this approach to the New Thought and New Age movements, as we have seen, both the Old Testament and the New Testament address it. Jesus speaks frequently of praying in this manner.

POWER ASKING

Think of a desire and ask for it carefully in the way discussed here. Use "I am" in your statement.

Ancient Age, Not New Age

In addition to my Diamond Approach teacher, I am fortunate to have a wise and mystical nun counsel me on spiritual direction. Sister Louise told me that this is actually an ancient, biblical way to pray. First you tell God what you desire and then give thanks for it occurring before it does. In this way, you are demonstrating to God the depth of your faith.

Prayer is used often when we are most desperate and unhappy. Undoubtedly, this is an important time to pray, and when God's grace enters the equation, no matter how you are feeling, your vibration rises. Although you can always turn to God, no matter what emotional state you are in, asking joyfully, with assurance and gratitude, requires you to give up the illusion of control and relax into Divine will.

Prayer is not begging, hoping, pleading, crying out, beseeching—but prayer is claiming, affirming, thanking and accepting, taking dominion over your desires—all stated in positive terms. The result of prayer is belief.

—Reverend Stretton Smith

Let us give thanks to God joyfully for what we are to receive as if we already have it.

Rejoice

When I listen to God, this is what I hear Her say:

I caress your face with the wind. I support your feet with the earth. I sing to you with the birds. You have much to be grateful for. Up the level of your gratitude and you will be rewarded. Be a light.

When I hear this, it makes me consider that even the simplest of gifts—like the wind, the earth, and the birds—are wonderful.

Rejoice in your life and in the gifts that are coming to you before they arrive. My children learned this lesson early in life. They give thanks to God for blessings in their day and then give thanks for what they want most. They approach this exercise with joy and enthusiasm. For them it is like play. As it should be.

My son says he enjoys receiving his gifts before they come. Recently, he wanted a new gaming system. Each night after thanking God for the blessings of his day, and giving thanks in advance for the gaming system he wanted, he lay in bed and "played" with his new gaming system with his hands and mind. Within a couple of months, a new babysitter offered to sell me this gaming system for a reduced price in time for my son's birthday.

Later when we talked about this, I realized my son had been rejoicing about the game's arrival before it had shown up. Even more important, Sanders knows that the manifestation of a gaming system is just the start to a life filled with miracles flowing in. Let us rejoice in the gifts we have received and in the gifts that are coming to us. When we walk in gratitude, we feel joy, generosity, and abundance. Merely the *discipline* of gratitude reshapes our lives and, as it does, other gifts start flowing in.

Oh Lord, the king rejoices in your strength.
How great is his joy at the victories you give!
You have granted him the desire of his heart
And have not withheld the request of his lips.
You have welcomed him with rich blessings
And placed a crown of pure gold on his head.
He asked you for life, and you gave it to him
length of days, for ever and ever.
Through the victories you gave, his glory is great;
You have bestowed on him splendor and majesty.
Surely you have granted him eternal blessings
And made him glad with the joy of your presence.
For the king trusts in the Lord;
Through his unfailing love of the Most High
He will not be shaken.

—Psalm 21:1–7

PART THREE

Find Your True Self

CHAPTER 11

Receiving Yourself

I decided I needed to climb a mountain to feel my power. I was feeling like a victim again. I had just ended the most profound relationship in my life up to that point because I realized it was unhealthy for me. Somehow, despite my best efforts, I had attracted the same relationship pattern, although it wasn't abusive this time. I could feel my power leaking away and I was sinking into the quicksand of victimhood.

To compound my grief, my former partner got into a serious relationship just seven days after we said good-bye—with a woman he had repeatedly told me he found attractive. I knew he was afraid of being alone, but it made me question the value of the whole relationship. I wondered whether he had loved me with the fierceness that I had loved him. Instead of remembering that I made the decision to end it, all of a sudden I felt like a jilted woman.

Worse, he, she, and I were involved in a dance community and I had to see them blissfully gazing at one another at the dances, a place where I usually felt so much joy. The first time I spun around in a dance to come face to face with them, I was raw with pain.

To reclaim my power, I chose the most rigorous hike in my area, a mountain called Old Rag. The ten-hour hike included serious rock scrambling in order to reach the summit. I had climbed it with my former boyfriend and that had felt like a victory. Now I was going to do it by myself with no strong man to hoist me up on rocks or pull me through crevices.

The morning of my planned hike it was rainy, but my guidance told me all was clear. I got to the mountain and it was magical, with the mist rising as the sun burned off the clouds. No one was there because of the earlier rain, perfect for my need for solitude. Despite the trail's popularity, I went the whole day without seeing more than five people.

I arrived at the first big rock and felt my confidence waver. I am a 5'4" woman with a father who is 6'6" and two brothers 6'4" and 6'5". Every man I had been in a serious relationship with, up to that point, was more than six feet tall. I spent my life literally running to catch up with their long legs and feeling dramatically smaller and shorter. I had a firmly embedded belief that I couldn't do the same things because I wasn't tall enough. I remember watching my ex-boyfriend pick up his long lanky leg, span what seemed like a six-foot-high ledge, and place his foot in a toehold on the rock. I looked at my short stubby legs and started to wonder how I could ever get up that rock.

I resolved I could do it. I started saying "You can do this," over and over again as a mantra. Soon I learned to use my height to my advantage. If I wedged my body up against the rock, I could use it for leverage to get over it. I scooted, slithered, and clung to the rocks. Places where I was too short to wedge myself in, I piled rocks to stand on.

Then I arrived at my Zen koan; the biggest challenge of my hike the previous time was when I had to leap over a small ravine to another rock. This was a place that had stalled many hikers. I remember hearing hiking partners urging each other on, sometimes for as long as an hour, until the hiker either leapt or turned around.

The last time, I had really struggled with it, measuring in my mind whether I could make the leap and analyzing how hurt I would get if I didn't make it. I finally had the realization that I would never move forward if I let my head make the decision. I suddenly announced, "I've got to get my head out of the way" and then leapt before I could think further. This time, I knew not to stop and contemplate. I just leapt—keeping my mind from telling me I could not do what many hikers and I had done before.

When I finally reached the summit hours later, I felt more powerful than ever. From my lookout, I could see clearly for miles around, and I had clarity on my inner landscape as well.

That rock-climbing episode pushed me to find new ways to overcome my fears and limitations. Every time I felt my grip loosen, or my ankles start to wobble as I walked over uneven rocks, I had the opportunity to challenge my old mental habits. When I caught myself creating a fear-filled picture of my ankle twisting and being stranded alone on a trail all night, I switched to the positive message "I have strong, healthy ankles, and they are going to carry me safely back to my car."

My Summit

Even better, my mind was as clear as the thin mountain air at the summit. I was no longer tortured by the image of my former boyfriend and his new love. No longer did a voice chatter away telling me what he was thinking, what she was thinking, what they were thinking of me, and what I was thinking about what they were thinking. No longer did I care about the elaborate story I had fabricated that claimed the blissful looks on their faces were because I had finally ended the relationship. What did I care if they believed I had kept them apart like two star-crossed lovers, separated in deference to my feelings and their own chivalry? (Oh, how I groan as I write this. I can't believe I went there!)

I did not finish walking down that mountain until 10:00 p.m. that night, after spending some time on the summit. But I came down a spiritual warrior who went into battle to fight for her power and emerged triumphant.

Receive All Your Power

What is your mountain that you need to climb in order to remember your power? You came to this Earth a strong, powerful being, packed into the body of a helpless little infant. Yet your power was so immense because you still remembered that you are a being of God and not separate from anything.

It is our feeling of separation, more than anything else, which makes us forget our power. If we can remember we are part of God, a Divine spark, which all the mystics throughout time have rhapsodized about, then we KNOW we are powerful.

It is through our unity that we remember how much power we have.

God is within and without us. God is all around us. *Our power is in yoking our little piece of God with the great vast God that surrounds us.* Jesus says, "Come follow me, my burden is sweet and my yoke is light."

If we only see God within us and we walk around thinking we are omnipotent, the Universe will bring us to our senses and remind us pointedly that we can't do it alone.

Even worse is when we see God as separate and outside us. Then we give up our Divine inheritance and our ability to create our lives. We see ourselves as little pieces of flotsam tossed around on the river of life with no power at all. It is when we link our spark with God's that we can receive all our power.

Rumi reminds us that we are spiritual beings having a human experience and urges us to join in union with God to feel our vastness:

> *No, we are the pearls from the bosom of the sea,*
> *it is there that we dwell:*
> *Otherwise how could the wave succeed to the*
> *wave that comes from the soul?*
> *The wave named "Am I not your Lord" has come,*
> *it has broken the vessel of the body;*
> *And when the vessel is broken, the vision comes back,*
> *and the union with Him.*

—Eva de Vitray-Meyerovitch, *Rumi and Sufism*

YOUR POWER

When have you experienced your power? Think about what represents your mountain. What was it about that experience that made you feel powerful?

Remember Your Victories

When I think of that mountain hike up Old Rag, I remember it as a victory. I can feel the sense of triumph in my body and the exhilaration in my heart. Call forth your victories. They can strengthen and fortify you and remind you who you are. It quickly takes you out of feeling like a victim and moves you into a victor status. The act of remembering them raises your vibration and attracts the best for you. I often ask clients to do this. I have them track back, like a DVD, to a moment in their life when they felt successful. I ask them to call up the feeling that went with that. I have them sit with this feeling of success and let it wash over them. We can feel it change their energy.

By feeling successes and victories from the past, it makes it easier to create new ones in the present, through both how we act and attract. My clients find they can change their energy from discouraged or hesitant to optimistic and confident by recalling the feeling of a victory.

One of my clients, who was running for political office, was getting negative feedback about his public appearances. Observers felt that he was nervous and tentative even when he did not feel that way. He could feel this perception draining energy away and shaking his confidence. I had him remember times when he served on boards on which he was a strong advocate and got feedback that his advocacy was appreciated. He remembered that his passion and commitment made a difference in people's lives and that he needed to convey this.

One client had a consulting business to which he was not attracting new clients. He was feeling insecure about his abilities and fearful about his dwindling client base. When he met with potential clients and they suggested a project, he would worry immediately whether he could do it. Before starting his business, he had always succeeded professionally and had risen to leadership positions quickly. I asked him to remember the string of successes in his professional life. He now walks into those meetings with the idea that "I can do this and do it well." His natural confidence, based on past victories, has brought in more clients.

Your victories may be remaining unscathed after leaving a bad job or the daily raising of small children. They may be excelling at a project or negotiating a good salary. Remember them. Savor them. And call them forth to fuel your power and shift your vibrations as you face new challenges.

VICTORY

List your past victories. How did they make you feel?

How Do You Value Yourself?

Your victories help you set your value, yet they are based in what you do. It is important to remember things you have done that were of value, but what about feeling like *you* are valuable? When you base all your worthiness on *doing* something, you don't allow yourself to feel worthy for just being.

Being is the essence of our soul. Our soul existed long before we received our bodies and will exist long after we leave our bodies. When placed in that context, it is vital to value your being. *Your being is going to be around a lot longer than your doing.*

If all your worthiness is linked to doing, you will never feel complete self-love because it will be based on the latest thing you did. Ray Dodd, author of *The Power of Belief*, believes we make agreements based on our beliefs. We learn that we are loved for a reason only. I will love you if . . . or I will love you when. . . .

Have you ever been around someone whose attitude toward you is "Yeah, you did do that for me in the past, but what are you going to do for me now?" They are exhausting to be around. There is no sense of gratitude or appreciation for who you are. It is all about what you can do for them. Your value hinges conditionally on the next thing you do.

You may realize how painful it is to be with someone like that, but make sure you are not doing this to yourself. It is time to start breaking the chains that bind you to this self-defeating, never-ending treadmill. Learning self-appreciation and unconditional love for yourself allows you truly to receive who you are.

SELF-VALUE

What qualities do you most value in yourself? Value yourself enough to come up with a list.

What We Are

We often forget who and what we are. It is like little Alice in *Alice in Wonderland*. She has always been resourceful, smart, and determined but she forgets this repeatedly. She faces constant challenges as she struggles to remember that she can save herself. At one point, when she grows huge, she still sees herself as weak. She doesn't realize that she is so big she could rule the land. In fact, her tears of powerlessness produce a flood—a powerful effect.

Alice also doesn't seem to realize that all the characters, including the Queen, are having such strong reactions to her because of their own fear. They are afraid of her power. Alice doesn't even know she has any power.

This happens to each of us, to some more than others. In looking back at my life, I was often seen as a leader when I felt insignificant. I was tentative and hesitant when people were waiting for me to lead. Imagine what a dichotomy this is—to be seen as big and powerful, yet feeling little and weak. People were waiting for me to lead as I was wondering why no one was leading.

You are the leader in your life. Don't sit around wondering who is leading. When you can't receive yourself as who you truly are, you can't let in all the good that is waiting for you.

When you first came into this world, you knew that you could create it. You knew that the spark of Divine inside you was one with all that was around you. You knew there was no separation between God and you. You felt the unity of all.

Remember who you are. Isn't it time you received yourself? Isn't it time that you accepted the gift of your true magnificence?

> **We think we are our bodies; we are not. We think we are our problems, or our ancestors, or our many identities.**
>
> **We are not. We are not our sex, or our illness, or our desire. We are not our loves, our pains, or our addictions.**
>
> **What we are is a piece of all that is, sired by the light, in order that the "isness" might experience itself greater than it was before.**
>
> **We are the embodiment of a love so vast, so incomprehensible, that we run from its power. Yet that power is what we are.**
>
> **We are the higher power that is greater than ourselves.**
>
> **We are a marvelous creation of mind in matter.**
>
> **We are the ongoingness and foreverness of everything that is.**
>
> **We are a portion of the infinite, a piece of God destined to wake up one day and remember just that.**
>
> **. . . We are what we look outside ourselves to find. We are the love we seek, the joy for which we yearn, the fervor of life we think we have lost. Our longing is but the pressing call of our soul to wake up, and to remember. This, then, is our grand journey home.**
>
> —Lynn Grabhorn, *The "Excuse Me, Your Life Is Waiting" Playbook*, page 1

How could you think you are anything less? There is a beautiful song we sometimes sing in my church, which has the lines "How could anyone ever tell you you were anything but beautiful? How could anyone ever tell you that you were anything but wise?" But that is the crux. People did tell us negative things about ourselves. They may have been subtle, like "You are not trying your best" or "Look how Sally does it," or they may have been brutal, like "You're an idiot" or "You can't do anything right." We took those messages on. WE TOOK THEM ON. And now we tell them to ourselves.

Your Inner Critic Is Not Who You Are

We all have an inner critic. It's the voice inside us running nonstop, giving us critical feedback. Some call it "the judge," others call it the superego, but it all comes down to a voice that is always second-guessing and criticizing you.

If you listen to this voice carefully, you will realize it is NOT YOU. Divide it out. It is the voice of your parent, teacher, or sibling, a voice that you took on years ago.

We take on this voice in childhood for good reason. It keeps us safe. It allows us to survive in our family and follow the rules of our parents so they will want to take care of us. Our parents would tell us the stove was hot and the inner critic would remind us each time we wanted to touch it. If we had parents who were neglectful and never kept us safe, then we discovered danger on our own. We touched the stove ourselves and our inner critic became even stronger from our experience.

As an adult, you don't NEED this voice. In fact, it gets in the way. It gets in the way of you receiving your magnificence. It gets in the way of you receiving your power. It gets in the way of you receiving God within and outside of you because you think less of yourself. And it gets in the way of attracting what you want because it lowers your vibration. You cannot have the vibration of love when you are engaging in self-hate. You cannot have the vibration of joy when you are puncturing your sense of self.

Who Tells You That You Are Not Worthy?

The voice of the inner critic tells you that you are not enough—that you are not good enough, smart enough, or admirable enough. This is the voice that worries what people will think of you. If the voice is harsh, it tells you that you are stupid, lazy, and deficient or deserve to be hated.

It is the voice that drives you to be perfect. It causes you to spend too much time picking out a gift at Christmas or decorating your house not because you WANT to, but because you feel you SHOULD. If you are a working mother, it tells you that you still have to keep house and cook the way your stay-at-home mom did. If a friend asks you to do something, it tells you that you are not a good friend if you need a little time for yourself. If you are a man, it is the voice that tells you that you should be able fix everything that breaks in your house or be the sole provider for your family. It is the voice that tells you what you SHOULD do to be a good person, instead of attuning to your FEELING of it.

I struggle with always running late. My inner critic has a running dialogue about it. My voice would beat me up if I was early because I could have been doing more work at home. My voice would beat me up when I was trying to leave the house because it was telling me about all the work left undone. My voice would beat me up when I got in the car because I realized I was going to be late and my voice beat me up as I ran into my meeting, with the final knockout blow that I was incompetent. Imagine starting a meeting with that vibration.

We need to protect ourselves from this voice. What if you heard an abusive person talking to someone else in that manner? What if it was your child being berated?

You wouldn't let someone talk to your child that way. Why do you let yourself be abused by this voice?

PROTECT YOUR CHILD

Imagine walking into a room and finding a small child being harshly berated. The child is frightened and is crying. Feel your protective energy come up. Go and stand between the child and the attacker. You are a shield for this child. Order the attacker out of the room. Then turn and comfort the child. Hold the child in your arms. Tell the child he or she is loved and perfect. Soothe this child. Feel your heart open to this precious beautiful little person. Look into his or her eyes and see a young version of yourself. Resolve to protect this child from attacks—whether external or by your inner critic.

Hushing the Inner Critic

Upon realizing this, most of us want to battle this inner critic. We want to banish it from our lives, and when it starts talking to us, we want to yell and scream at it. What do you think this does for your vibration? What do you think the focus on it will cause? It will cause it to EXPAND! That is the last thing we want it to do.

An effective way to deal with your inner critic is merely to turn to it and say, "Thanks for sharing," in the way you would talk to an annoying relative to whom you don't give much credence. When it really bugs you, you can ask it to take a walk. As a mother, I often enjoy visualizing mine taking a time-out.

I coach a writer who had an inner critic that harassed her at bookstores. She was frustrated by it because she believed in buying books to support other writers, she had a budget she never went over, and she even sold or gave away books periodically to make room for new selections. I suggested that she tell her inner critic as she entered the bookstore that it had to stay outside. Now I know this sounds goofy—to tell an imaginary voice in your head to stay outside!—but it worked. She called me up, ecstatic that the inner critic had stayed outside and she had been able to have an enjoyable buying experience.

Your Yelling Voice Stops Your Success

When I was in China, in a town near Xi'an, I spoke to four hundred high school students about setting goals and being successful. The students were on vacation but almost all of them showed up for my speech because the school asked them to. (Imagine that in the United States!) China has a harsh system in which public humiliation is used to motivate students. Every student's grades are published so all students can see who is succeeding and who is failing. Parents push their children hard and teachers are critical.

These students were expecting a speech about how they needed to push harder to be successful. They expected me to talk to them about reaching goals and staying focused. I did speak to them briefly on these topics. But then I told them that to be truly successful, they had to believe in themselves. That they could only go so far in noting what they did wrong and working harder to get it right. I shared with them that true success comes from being able to celebrate what we do right and replicate it on a grander scale.

I talked with them about this inner judge that always makes us wrong. So they could understand, I phrased it in terms of the yelling voice that hounds them all day long. I told them that this voice might initially help them toward success, but it would inevitably stop them from really succeeding.

The students sat there stunned. No one had ever told them that this voice gets in the way of their success. No one had told them that this voice is NOT really them—it is not WHO they are. I told them that it is just a voice. We can't silence it but we can turn the volume down. I added that the "who" we truly are comes from our hearts and souls, not the voice in our head that puts us down.

At the end of my speech, fifty students wanting my autograph, some crying with relief or asking for advice, mobbed me. I had a teacher come up to me, say that what I said went totally against all she had been taught, and that she was thankful for a new way. She was going to start using this concept to guide her students in the classroom.

My father and the other Chinese college students traveling with us had gone outside at the end of my speech. After about twenty minutes, my father turned around and asked where I was. They found me surrounded by a tight circle of students wanting to know more about how to turn this voice down.

The Inner Critic Doesn't Want You to Receive

Remember the greatest challenge to the Law of Attraction is learning how to receive. The largest block to a relationship with God is being able to receive. The inner critic doesn't want you to receive because that would be an acknowledgment that you *are* worthy. If you are worthy, you won't need the inner critic to tell you what to do and it will lose its power over you. This is threatening to the voice that has ruled you for much of your life.

If life is a river, the inner critic wants you to row upstream. It tells you that it is too easy to go downstream and that you are lazy for wanting a life that flows. Yet learning to go downstream is all about attracting and allowing what you want in your life. When you can receive the river current in the direction it comes to you, instead of fighting it, then you start to flow *easefully* through your life.

Why not take the paddle away from the inner critic and *you* determine the direction you wish to go?

INNER CRITIC CHATTER

In your worst moments, what does your inner critic say about you? Make a list. For each negative criticism write a positive affirmation to counteract it. For example, if you say "I'm lazy," write a positive affirmation such as "I work with integrity and dedication and I allow myself time to rest."

Rejecting Yourself

The opposite of not receiving yourself is rejecting yourself. Think about it for a minute. If you cannot receive yourself, then you reject who you are. These stark words give me pause. By rejecting yourself, you block all goodness that might come to you. You deny yourself all the gifts under the Christmas tree that have your name on them. You firebomb the bridge so that no supply trucks can get to you. You dam up your river so that you cannot flow down it.

Once you can objectively listen to your inner critic, you will hear that all the messages have to do with rejecting who you are. It is essential to turn down the volume on this self-hate and have a discipline of self-love so you can learn to receive yourself.

I have found, in my coaching practice, that the underlying belief sabotaging my clients from reaching their goals is "I am not worthy." None of us, me included, have completely healed this wound. It is our life's work and it affects our relationship with God.

This is the root of every problem you experience in your life—for you do not consider yourself worthy enough to be spoken to by God. Good heavens, how can you ever expect to hear My voice if you don't imagine yourself deserving enough to even be spoken to?

—Neale Donald Walsch, *Conversations with God, Book 1,* page 69

I often recommend Louise Hay's book *You Can Heal Your Life* to clients to accelerate their healing. Her affirmations and exercises focus on readers learning to love and accept themselves:

The innermost belief for everyone I have worked with is always, I'm not good enough. All . . . you have experienced, . . . [heard], and . . . read form a filter of belief through which you interpret everything. Its expression is the conversation you hear chattering in your mind. . . . (page 6)

Louise Hay was one of the forerunners in teaching the Law of Attraction to our generation. As she states it:

The Universe totally supports every thought we choose to think and to believe. . . . Whatever these beliefs are, they will be recreated as experiences as we grow up. However, . . . *the point of power is always in the present moment.* Changes can begin in this moment. (page 17)

Changes can begin this moment. You might say, "Oh, this doesn't apply to me. I really love myself." Look deeper. Nearly all, if not all, of us have some area in which we have rejected ourselves. I believe that rejecting ourselves is ungodly. Rejecting ourselves stems from deep wounds, usually from childhood, but they must be addressed before you can fully receive.

Receiving Yourself as Your Most Precious Child

I found it easier to start accepting myself when I viewed myself as my most precious child. I was able to activate my strong nurturing energy and my mama-tiger protective side in service of myself. Finding the energy of the good parent within us helps us take better care of ourselves.

I urge clients to try to access their inner parent so they can better nurture and protect the precious child who is inside them. If they can create their own image of a parent who is healthy, protective, and unconditionally loving, it helps them set better boundaries in their lives.

When life is particularly stressful and the inner critic starts beating them up, I suggest that they remember the picture of this voice saying ugly things to a child. I ask them to pull up the energy of the "good parent" to protect themselves.

Generate for yourself unconditional love, the way you would love a child who is precious to you.

What God says to me about this is:

When people reject themselves, they reject me. That is so important for people to hear and get. They reject the very essence of who I am. This is the greatest sin. Jesus came to teach people to embrace themselves, to embrace their lives. Receive yourself so you can receive me.

RECEIVE YOUR PRECIOUS CHILD

Visualize yourself as a precious child surrounded by love.
Say: "I receive myself as a precious child of God."

Receive Yourself as You Receive Me

"Receive yourself so you can receive me." Stop for a minute and reflect on what that means. We are charged with learning how to love ourselves. Instead of the old-school theory that we are defective and not worthy of God, but He loves us anyway, this message challenges us to rethink the commandment "Love thy neighbor as thyself." The verse goes both ways. Not only are we charged with loving our neighbor, we are charged with loving ourselves. If we reject ourselves, if we hate some part of ourselves, then we CANNOT love our neighbor as ourselves because we do not love ourselves.

Imagine how a woman who suffers from anorexia sees herself. She looks in the mirror and cannot see the skeleton that is her body. Instead, she sees layers of fat.

What are you erroneously seeing about yourself? Are you like a wealthy person, bedecked with expensive diamonds, yet when you look at them, all you see is cubic zirconia? Or, even worse, a lump of coal?

When you feel this rejection of yourself come up, it is imperative to retrain the way you think. When you look in the mirror, you should see yourself as the jewel you are. Remember, you are actually retraining your brain's neuropathways. You need, instead, to reframe your thought immediately. Reach for the positive about yourself. Affirm that you are worthy and that you accept yourself. Make the choice in each moment.

We have spent a lifetime learning not to value and love ourselves. Create a discipline of self-love. This is different from self-absorption or valuing yourself above others. Instead, find ways to affirm and appreciate yourself.

When people come to me with a problem, I don't care what it is . . . there is only one thing I ever work on, and that is LOVING THE SELF. . . . when we really love, accept, and APPROVE OF OURSELVES EXACTLY AS WE ARE, then everything in life works.

—Louise Hay, *You Can Heal Your Life*, page 8

A DISCIPLINE OF SELF-LOVE

Make a list of what you can do to create a daily discipline of self-love. For example, you can start each day with the statement "I love myself" or when you look in the mirror you can tell yourself that you are beautiful and loved. Stretch past your comfort zone.

Welcome Yourself Home

To receive goodness into your life, you must believe that you are good. To be able to fully commune with God with no blocks, you must be able to love yourself. Remember, to reject yourself is to reject the spark of God in you, for Jesus says, "I am in my Father and you are in me, and I am in you."

When I listen, I hear God tell me:

Choose to be in a place where you can see my beauty and your beauty and the beauty of the world.

See this beautiful precious child receiving all the beauty that life has to offer. Receiving that you are who you think you are at your highest grandest level. Welcome yourself into your life! Welcome yourself home, like the father of the prodigal son.

CHAPTER 12

Receiving Your Highest Energy

I spent a week in solitude praying, meditating, and writing at the cabin. My prayer was to be washed clean of all that blocked me from my Highest Self and from hearing God's voice. I wanted to be free of the static and negativity that dragged my energy down.

As the week progressed, the constant sound of the twin streams running reminded me of the flow of life. Something was flowing through me as if I were being baptized anew. I often felt dizzy, light-headed. There were times when I burst into sudden tears as tenderness arose in me. The stars on a velvety black sky, the beauty of the mountains, the vulnerability of a baby fawn, and the whirl of a hummingbird's wings all moved me deeply.

One morning, when I awoke, I felt different. I was both lighter and more solid. I felt a lightness radiating from inside me and I felt more grounded in my body. There was a weightiness and sense of awareness in my body, especially my arms and legs, more pronounced than before. For the first time, I felt consistently present in the moment.

My energy had shifted. I felt a healing take hold in my spirit and with it a more well-defined desire to be a healer.

Call forth the highest version of yourself. Stretch into the energy of who you want to be. Do this through seeing yourself already as the spiritual being that you aspire to be. Know that at some level you are there already.

Do this in honor of God and yourself. Give thanks for the person you are and the person that you envision yourself being. In my morning meditation ritual, I used to thank God for my children, naming them as my greatest gift. One day I realized I was short-changing them if I could not see myself as my greatest gift. Now I thank God for me—for all the potential that I have, the gifts I have, and my blemishes. As much as I resist them, as much as I anguish about my flaws, they are mine. Part of being able to address and transcend them requires me to forgive myself for having flaws. Forgiveness is the most intense form of self-love.

My wise Diamond Approach teacher pointed out to me that by putting myself first, I was honoring my children. He suggested that I model to them, in a world full of self-loathing and ego grandiosity, the humility and compassion of authentically loving one's self. By doing this, I love them more deeply.

Making Room in Your Heart

Not only must we forgive our imperfections, we must also forgive others their flaws. Old resentments are burdens that drag down our energy. *Radical Forgiveness,* by Colin Tipping, helped change my life because he urges us not only to forgive those who hurt us, but also to consider that we may have formed soul agreements with these individuals before we were born, to help us grow. His radical idea is that there is, really, nothing to forgive. Since most of us don't feel that way, however, Tipping urges us to examine our old injuries and be willing to consider the possibility of forgiving those who caused them. By doing so, we are moved toward forgiveness.

When we forgive, we do so not for others but for ourselves, so we no longer drag that burden around with us. To forgive is to cut ourselves free from that old hurt; otherwise we continue to let old wounds from the past have power over our present and future.

As we start a forgiveness practice, we soon discover that it is not only the big hurts we need to forgive, but also the everyday resentments. Briefly review your day each evening and notice the small, subtle ways you resent others. Letting these resentments go allows you to start your next day with clean energy.

Forgiveness lets us start fresh—not by losing the discernment to protect ourselves from future injury—but by energetically inviting people to manifest as their Highest Selves. The more we see others' Highest Selves—even when they are not acting from that place—the more they show up that way. They are released from our image of their old selves, and they can make a choice to meet our higher expectations.

Forgiving ourselves and others takes courage. It is a job for a spiritual warrior. In doing so, we move from victim to hero because we break the patterns that hold us down.

CLEAR NEGATIVE ENERGY

Take some time each day to clear the clutter of negative feelings that has built up. This includes old resentments, pent-up feelings, and all the negative self-talk. Forgive others and yourself.

The Seductiveness of Chaos

Our energy is also impacted by the chaos in our lives and our reaction to it. I have had a lifelong pattern of attracting chaos. I've worked a lot on this. I see why I did this—growing up I had a lot of chaos. I see how my attention deficit disorder plays into my chaos and how I believe on some level that it is exciting to have chaos. I thought I had it conquered after much introspection, self-discovery, and action steps toward a smoother life. Yet chaos kept showing up in my life.

I realized that, despite the many reasons crisis kept reoccurring in my life, at some level I was still inviting it in. This was disheartening to me because, believe me, I was OVER chaos. I was like a woman initially seduced by the excitement of a bad boy lover, who has grown older and wiser and no longer falls for the seduction because she sees the high cost.

I don't want any more chaos. I was begging God for a life full of ease, grace, and flow. Still, more chaos kept arising. I stopped begging, realizing that it was a strong "don't want" that would surely pull in more. I affirmed I could live a life of ease, grace, and flow.

I visualized a smooth life. Yet periodically, chaos would show up like an uninvited guest.

Certainly, I was doing things that helped create the chaos. I didn't attend to details, such as pay bills on time, organize my papers so I could find everything I needed to keep my bills in line, keep my house tidy, and arrive on time. These bad habits contributed mightily to the chaos created. I started focusing tremendous energy on getting these under control.

I hired an assistant with an accounting background to help me organize my finances.

I worked with a professional organizer.

I hired a cleaning team who was willing to come in initially once a month because that is what I could afford.

I started teaching my kids to help around the house. These were all areas that I had been working on for years, but I faced them with new vigor.

I also had to rein in my tendency to have too much going on and I had to reframe how I structured my day. Unlike a person who finds "Seize the day" inspiring, I found it a burden. A mantra that worked for me much better is "My life is long." I relaxed and realized I don't have to do it all in one day or even one year. I starting cutting down on what I did. I slowed down and focused more intensely on my goals.

Life kept getting better and better. Amazing opportunities arose repeatedly. I could feel myself moving into wisdom and clarity. And despite this, chaos kept coming.

I prayed about it, went to therapy about it, and worked on it in workshops and spiritual retreats.

I meditated each morning, which helped center me and connect me with God.

I did affirmations. I went to healers. Still chaos kept coming.

And then one day I had a profound shift. Chaos came and I just watched it. I didn't identify with it. I maneuvered through it, blessing all that helped me work around it. I chose not to focus on it. I changed my relationship with chaos and then the chaos changed. It stopped showing up as much, and when it did, it was a smaller version with solutions that arose to address the challenge.

For example, soon after this shift, I was running late for a spiritual retreat and I had been assigned to handle the room assignments. As I was loading my car, a wasp got under my skirt and stung me three times. I thought I got it out. An hour into the ride it turns out it was still there and it stung me another four times. Trying not to wreck my car, I pulled up my skirt and out came the wasp. Distracted, I made a wrong turn.

Yet I trusted that all would work out. Soon I found a road that would enable me to cut back over and get to my desired location. I did not resist the pain of the stings, but I chose not to focus on it. My mistake meant I was running behind by almost an hour. I knew all those people were waiting for me and were unable to unpack in their rooms until I arrived with their room assignments. It was a time ripe for my inner critic to unload on me about how people were counting on me and how I had failed them. In times past, I would have pictured them grumbling about me and been fearful of their anger. I chose not to follow that old self-defeating pattern. Instead, I chose to remember that these were kind, loving people who enjoyed the beauty of the retreat center and each other's company.

When I arrived, that is exactly what they were doing. They were relaxed; some catching up with each other, and some walking on the beautiful grounds or sitting on the large porch. I told my story, but not defensively, just merely to share. Before, I would have cranked it up to illustrate that I had a good reason for arriving late, and projected "poor little me, what I went through to get here, so please don't be angry with me." This time I told it with some humor and insight, but I WASN'T the story. It was just *a* story. I kept my equilibrium and nothing lowered my vibration. Even the wasp stings gave me little pain.

My reward was that it no longer felt like chaos had a hold over me. In fact, it no longer feels like chaos visits me. Instead, when problems occur, it is an opportunity for me to affirm my resourcefulness and ability to problem-solve.

SEDUCED BY CHAOS

Have you been seduced by chaos? If you have been or still are, what is it that you get out of the experience? Do you become a drama king or queen when chaos appears? Does chaos make you feel like a victim? Make a list of five positive empowered ways to respond to chaos.

The Hero's Quest

Fairytales have heroes who fight dragons, scale towers, and pull the sword from the stone. Victims wait for a hero to rescue them instead of becoming their own hero.

You know the tale. Someone normal and regular is sent on a journey to face obstacles and challenges. As she transforms into a hero, she often realizes that what she is questing for has always resided within her.

Think of Aragorn, when he was still Strider the Ranger from *The Lord of the Rings,* right before he becomes a leader in battle. The Elfin king presents him a sword from his royal ancestors and challenges him to become "the man you were born to be."

We all have a divine royal heritage. Be the man or woman you were born to be. This is your life you are fighting for! We are talking about nothing less than living the life you want, not settling for a life you have that leaves you depressed and uninspired. Even though you are not at risk of dying, you are at risk of LOSING your life if you can't fight for it! Be your own hero.

Have Light Energy Not Dark Energy

Embrace light and love. Make sure you are a hero, not an antihero. The antihero has become a mainstay of popular culture. Antihero personas abound in television and movies—Clint Eastwood in Dirty Harry or Anakin gone bad as Darth Vader. They are complex, interesting, and oh, so dark.

Antiheroes feel victimized so they become the predator. As I wrote this, three hours away at Virginia Tech University in Blacksburg, thirty-two people lost their lives because a young man who saw himself as a victim was actually a predator. Now it is clear he was mentally ill, yet he was not a bullied child who was fighting back. Professors and students had reached out to him repeatedly. His predator side surfaced once before when he stalked female students. His killing rampage appeared well thought out and coolly calculated. The challenge for those who were victimized by him is to resist being defined as a victim for the rest of their lives, or to become so fearful and angry that *they* turn into a predator. In the aftermath of the massacre, it was impressive to hear how empowered, wise, and loving so many of the young students were. Instead of being sucked into the darkness of another's twisted hatred, they were choosing to be in the light.

Sometimes heroes have a dark, shadow side, living as a tormented superhero, whether Batman, the X-Men, or the Incredible Hulk. Although they do good things, they have a sad energy that keeps them locked into a being seen as the enemy even when they save lives.

Choosing to be dark energy or light energy isn't dependent on one's life circumstances. After all, Superman was an orphan whose whole planet and race expired. He loved a woman who couldn't see his true self. Yet he has a positive energy and is one of the few superheroes who can fly on his own power.

Choose Light Not Dark

My whole life I have been attracted to dark people. I told myself that, as in the Greek tragedies, dark people were more complex and interesting. This is not so.

Dark, complex people wear me out. The first big love of my life once told me that it is a curse to be intelligent because then you are truly aware of how difficult life is. He believed it is better to be born stupid and unaware so you won't realize how bad things really are. What a tragic and mistaken belief system, one that becomes self-fulfilling. Tragedies are hard to explain, as is a difficult life. Yet sometimes a higher good is served, and our test is what energy we choose. The Dalai Lama is neither stupid nor unaware, yet his life has not been easy. He lost his country and many of his people, and saw his religion oppressed. Yet he does not view life as a struggle, but rather, a blessing. Because of his energy and leadership, he is a blessing to the entire world.

Oprah Winfrey faced huge challenges in her life, yet her energy makes her stand out like a beacon among talk TV personalities. The American public is more open and enlightened because of her influence.

Nelson Mandela could have viewed life as a struggle, spending twenty-seven years in prison, yet he holds the energy of strength, compassion, forgiveness, and wisdom. South Africa would not be the same without his peaceful leadership.

ENERGY ROLE MODELS

Who are people you admire? List their qualities. What kind of energy do they hold? Remember, if you can recognize it in others, it means you possess it also.

Being the Energy You Want

You can choose to hold your energy like people you admire hold theirs. You can *be* the energy you want. One way to do this is to model after others you admire. Another way is to try on the energy you want, as if trying on a new outfit. Just as aspiring executives are told to dress to feel like they are executive material, you can try on the energy you want to be. You will start to become it.

Have you ever played a sport? The coach may help you master a skill by moving your body. I have seen golf pros adjust a golfer's stance or swing so he or she can feel how to get it right.

In yoga class, the teacher walks around and makes adjustments by pushing or pulling the student's body into the correct position.

In my belly dance class, my teacher will put her hand on my hips and move me so I can feel how to do a dance step correctly.

By having someone move you into a correct position, you are able to feel a new way of being. It gives your body new information that you can't access by watching others and trying to mimic them. The same goes for energy. You can learn to feel your power by accessing the energy of something else that is powerful. This is when using an archetype is helpful.

Archetypes are symbols. Because archetypes represent a part of ourselves, they allow us to change ourselves. They are like bookmarks, reminding us of what we already know but have forgotten. It is a way to step into another role, to enter an energy field, and experience what it feels like.

By identifying with one or more archetypes, we can identify our own nature and remember all that we are. We can use these archetypes as a spiritual guide to the discovery of self. Carl Jung believed that archetypes reside in the collective unconscious, which is why they are universally recognized and contained, to a greater or lesser degree, within the psyche of every person. We see archetypes in myths, fairytales, literature, and movies—and powerfully in religious imagery. Just like the different faces of God, archetypes make accessible the psyche's capacity to imagine unseen forces. Thus, these archetypes help the person connect to the Eternal; they make great mysteries more accessible by providing multiple images.

As a woman who often felt powerless, finding strong archetypes helped me get a visceral sense of power. Accessing the archetypal energy of a warrior allowed me to reframe my perception of myself. Instead of feeling victimized, I could see myself protecting my boundaries with strength and courage.

I took up fencing, karate, and archery—warrior skills. I started a small collection of swords so that I could pick up a sword and really feel the strength and power of a warrior. I originally found it intimidating to hold such a deadly weapon, but I also felt an energy shift in me. Swords are metaphors for me about staying strong, not as an aggressor, but instead based in my own power and integrity.

Fuel the Feeling

Yet even with a sword in my hand, sometimes I need to remember other victories to fuel the feeling of power. I used to take fencing classes with an old boyfriend and he and I would sometimes spar at home with wooden swords. Once, when I was new at it, he backed me into a corner. He and I instantly knew it was a bad dynamic, one that triggered old feelings of disempowerment.

I started to feel weak and powerless immediately, and waves of exhaustion washed over me. I could feel myself collapsing, unable to feel my power, like the way I'd felt in my marriage. But then something happened that caused a profound shift in me, not only in that moment, but also in the knowledge that I could shift my energy quickly by remembering my victories. I remembered that I had run four miles earlier that week while training for a race. I had not run since high school, twenty-four years before, so that distance was significant for me. I looked at him and yelled, "I just ran four miles. I am not getting backed into a corner."

I felt energy surge through me in that moment. It was like rocket fuel in me. I charged out of that corner with so much strength that it took him, and me, aback. Soon he was the one cornered, but happy that I had remembered my warrior spirit.

Access Your Power through an Archetype

This technique is so powerful that I often use archetypes with my clients so that they can stretch into a new way of being. When they share with me some of their struggles, I am quickly able to feel the energy they need to access. When I first introduce clients to the concept of archetypes, I usually confine it to the four used in John Weir Perry's book *Lord of the Four Quarters:* sovereign, warrior, lover, and magician.

There are many archetypes to choose from, however, such as those discussed in two excellent books: *The Hero Within,* by Carol Pearson; and *Sacred Contracts,* by Caroline Myss. I also urge clients to create their own archetypes.

The four basic archetypes of sovereign, warrior, lover, and magician can help us balance our energy and stretch into new ways of being. These energies help transform our weak areas into strengths. Our ability to become a higher energy is related directly to living as our Highest Self.

A Sovereign's Energy

I often work with managers who have problems delegating and supervising employees. With these clients, I urge them to feel a sovereign's energy. I remind them that they are the boss and to pull up the best sense of a sovereign—one who can survey the land, see the big picture, create a vision and goals, and delegate so the entire country (company, organization) can succeed. The coaching homework I assign these managers is to find a representation of a king or queen for their desks.

Women managers, who sometimes struggle to balance the desire for harmony with strong leadership, find the image of a queen's energy empowering. One woman client was promoted to lead an office during conflict because her leadership ability was valued. She felt insecure inside, however. Remembering that she had a queen's energy helped her transition into this new role and start owning it.

Another client had a boss who did not see her potential and she felt undervalued. When an opportunity for promotion arose, she was overlooked although she was clearly capable. I suggested that it was time to start looking for a new job and to get a little toy queen for her desk to remind her of her value. She went on to head up a non-profit company with a million-dollar budget.

A couple of male CEOs who are clients still act like the warriors they had to be to rise to the top. As their coach, I have to remind them that it is time to start accessing their king energy to be wise and strong leaders, and to realize that they no longer have to fight in every situation.

When I sent one young man out to find a king toy, he felt that all the kings looked weak and in his words "girly." He insisted on buying a king in armor that had a drawn sword. I observed that part of his problem was that he felt he needed to fight in every situation. I urged him to examine his resistance to buying a king without a weapon.

Sovereigns know they are worthy of a relationship with God. They also have the authority to confer blessings on others. Take these qualities on for yourself.

A SOVEREIGN'S ENERGY

Imagine yourself as a king or queen sitting on your throne surveying your country. Feel the confidence of being regal and wise. You are making decisions that will impact the good of many. When you walk into the room, people feel your power and compassion. See a version of yourself standing in front of you, the sovereign. Put your hand on the shoulder of this image of you and confer a blessing.

A Warrior's Energy

Many people do not feel comfortable in conflict or even being assertive. Some of my clients need to own their ability to fight like a warrior and set a strong boundary. I ask them if their **life is worth** fighting for so they can have the life they want—for usually, this is really what we are working on in coaching. When framed that way, clients are able to start making the shift to be assertive or set priorities. Often these clients pride themselves on their ability to get along, but feel others often take advantage of them.

I understand this feeling oh too well! The warrior in all of us knows that there are times we need to fight for a greater good. This is an energy I have had to work on a lot—hence my swords, fencing classes, archery, and karate. My desk is filled with female warriors from women pirates to Amazons to queens and princesses with swords.

As we move toward God, the image of a spiritual warrior is powerful. We must have the discipline and perseverance of a warrior and the strength to make a direct connection.

A WARRIOR'S ENERGY

Visualize yourself as a warrior with a sword. You have strength and clarity and can cut through all that doesn't serve you. You are able to set firm boundaries and protect yourself and others. Feel the power that comes from strength and clarity. Imagine the feeling of a sharp sword in your hand. See yourself as a force to be reckoned with. Now call up the image of a spiritual warrior. Sense the dedication, passion, and courage this requires. Consider how spiritual warriors use their energy on their spiritual journey home.

A Lover's Energy

Often people in high-level executive jobs have sacrificed their personal lives to succeed in their careers. They need a lover's energy to discover their heart's desire and to create loving relationships. They also need a lover's energy to remember to take time for themselves. The image of a mother who loves freely or a couple in love helps remind them to love themselves with that same fervor. Many people need to learn self-care so they have enough to give to others. Almost all of us need to work on self-love, a mental place where we can learn to accept and celebrate ourselves the way a devoted lover might dote on us.

A lover's energy is important to access when you want to receive God fully into your life. The softening that you feel when you first fall in love, that sense of bliss and contentment, is there in your relationship with God. God accepts and celebrates who you are, so when you are unable to do this for yourself, you reject this gift. Like a lover, you need to open your embrace so that God can fully love you. The lover archetype in divine communion is personified by Rumi's relationship with God:

> *In a dream last night I saw*
> *an ancient one in the garden of love,*
> *beckoning with his hand, saying, "Come here."*
> *On this path, Love is the emerald,*
> *the beautiful green that wards off dragonsnough,*
> *I am losing myself.*

—from Eva de Vitray-Meyerovitch, *Rumi and Sufism*

A LOVER'S ENERGY

Recall a time when you were in love. Remember how it felt to merge into another and to soften your heart. Allow this feeling to sweep over you. Maybe you once felt this merging as a child or as a parent holding an infant in your arms. Feel your heart become like melted butter. Melt into the feeling of being one with the Beloved.

A Magician's Energy

The magician archetype is powerful for attracting and creating. Some of my clients feel trapped in their jobs. I ask them to use the magician's energy to create a new life for themselves. I remind them that it is within their power to create what they want in their lives if they can let go of their old belief systems and the sense of "should" that keeps them trapped. Among the changes my clients have made are: taking six months off to hike the Appalachian Trail, moving to Paris to be an actress, starting a business, and finding a wonderful Victorian home in a rural village and retiring early. These clients accessed the power of the magician to go far beyond where they thought they would end up. Some have wizard toys or fairies on their desks to remind them of their ability to create. I have a lovely fairy godmother with a wand on my desk.

A MAGICIAN'S ENERGY

See yourself as a magician. Picture yourself in a magician's cape with a wand being able to create magic in your life. As you use the wand, sparkles of light fly from it. Feel the power of being able to create magic and manifest. See things you desire appear before your eyes.

Now feel yourself as merely a channel for the magic. Experience a divine energy flowing through you as you produce your magic.

Four Energies for a Life of Creation

All four of these energies—the warrior, the lover, the sovereign, and the magician—help us fully receive ourselves and live in balance. Each energy helps us create our lives through the Law of Attraction and a new relationship with God.

To recap: The sovereign lives in the knowledge that the landscape of our lives is our territory and that we have the ability to give and receive great blessings. A sovereign understands that we are deserving of a relationship with God and that God is our partner in creation.

A warrior reminds us to protect ourselves and to set healthy boundaries as a way to care for ourselves. The warrior is needed to stay steadfast in our quest for God and to withstand the naysayers who do not believe we can create our lives. A spiritual warrior's courage allows us to hold fast to our vision and to endure the intensity that a relationship with God brings.

Love, represented by the lover, is the key ingredient for the Law to operate through. Remember, throughout history, the Law of Attraction has been called the Law of Love. When we sink into the bliss of God's love, all of life seems to flow.

And the magician is, of course, the one who believes in magic. As magicians, we are able to create and manifest. A wise magician also knows that we are only channels through which the Divine flows.

These archetypes represent energies that are already inside us. We have all the wisdom, strength, love, and creative powers we need. We just need to remember these energies are there within us and learn to access them.

God Energy

The energy we emit is a combination of our conscious and unconscious thoughts, feelings, and actions. Our energy can be filled with emotional debris from old wounds, can be static from conflicting emotions and subconscious beliefs, and can be colored by the way we act out old patterns. We can slowly sort out old beliefs, heal old wounds, and learn to know ourselves. We can see where we need to access different types of energy so that we can be whole and powerful. As we do, we stretch toward our Highest Self and receive our highest energy.

To aspire to our Highest Self is to access God's energy within us. Spiritual traditions all approach this goal, albeit with different strategies. The Buddhists talk of right livelihood, right mind, and right action. Christians often ask themselves, "What would Jesus do?" The Jesuits' mantra that frames every small action is "God's highest glory." Centering prayer and mantras allow us to find stillness so we can feel God. Some meditation practices focus on having the heart open; others have us observe all that arises in the mind and body so that we truly know ourselves and our motivations. Some meditations cultivate mindfulness so we are fully present in the moment. All these are attempts to draw us not only closer to God, but also to help us be more like God.

> **As a contemporary mystic, you are measured by the quality of attitude you bring to all your tasks, by your capacity to be a model of generosity, and by challenging the fear that there is not enough to go around in this world— whether that is money, love, food, fame, power, attention, success or social position . . . mindful that every second offers a choice either to channel grace or to withhold it.**
>
> —Caroline Myss, *Entering the Castle,* page 29

Imagine if we were to be mindful that every second offers a choice to either channel grace or withhold it? If we could frame each day with the intention as a channel of grace, not only would our lives be filled with blessings, but we would also be a blessing in others' lives.

God plus you equals a power life full of joy, meaning, and purpose. To honor yourself is a way to honor God, as you are God's living temple. When we move toward Who We Really Are, instead of who we have been showing up as, our life is extraordinary.

CHAPTER 13

Knowing God
by Knowing Yourself

By the time I was an executive coach, I had identified self-defeating behaviors and was consciously trying to unhook from my addictive patterns. I was skilled at helping others do the same. Yet my most powerful lesson in the power of negative attraction came during one three-week crisis.

The same week I landed in jail, my house went into foreclosure proceedings. I was still reeling from being handcuffed in front of my children and spending the night in jail when I received the legal papers.

Though carrying around a sick feeling in the pit of my stomach, I had been in denial about the reality of the foreclosure happening. A big institutional client was three months behind in paying me a large sum of money, a sum that I needed for house payments.

For the first two months, I was like an ostrich in the sand. I buried my head in denial, ignored the calls and letters from the mortgage company, and went to the mailbox every day looking for my money. I was busy manifesting book deals, lectures, and an already paid for vacation with my kids—but little money.

The third month, I scraped together close to a full payment, but the mortgage company would have none of that. They held my check without cashing it and put my house into foreclosure proceedings, without notifying me until a week before the sale.

I frantically fixed the situation within five days before I was scheduled to leave with my father for Peru where we were both presenting papers at a conference. My topic was on how I used the archetype of a sword in coaching women to feel more powerful, something I was having trouble accessing in that moment.

I was painfully aware of the irony. I had attracted a crisis of a seismic magnitude for a success coach who helped people change self-defeating behavior. I felt estranged from myself and from my Source.

Dr. Candace Pert has done research on the molecules of emotion. She discovered that our brains get an addictive "hit" if we repeat an old pattern, regardless of whether it is healthy for us—heroin for the brain. We have an addictive pull to revert to an old way because it feels good, even if we *want* to act and be different. The good news is that we can repattern the neuropathways in our brain through conscious decisions and the repetition of new choices.

It is often said that who we are is a well-guarded secret, but the secret is well guarded not by a dragon, not by lions, but by our patterns. These old patterns twist around our soul, threatening to choke off our connection with our Source. They evolve from a lifetime of experiences and in reaction to how we have been hurt. Old woundings build up like scar tissue until Who We Really Are becomes obscured.

Traveling the Homeland

To know God fully, we must know ourselves. Our ego and old addictive patterns get in the way of God's voice and of our Highest Self. Once we can see clearly what drives us, we can make new choices.

Philosophers throughout the ages talk about the value of self-observation. Plato urged us to live the examined life. Sufis talk about this in terms of "traveling the homeland." We travel in our interior world so that we might know ourselves better. By knowing ourselves better, we understand why we act the way we do and how we block ourselves from greatness.

Thich Nhat Hanh, the venerated Vietnamese monk and spiritual leader, observes that both Buddha and Jesus realized that life is filled with suffering and both made every effort to offer a way out. Hanh advises that if we can be alone and quiet and look deeply into the nature of our suffering, *we will find a way out.*

Following the Current

A. H. Almaas, the founder of the Diamond Approach Work and author of *Spacecruiser Inquiry: True Guidance for the Inner Journey,* among other books, urges us to follow the current of our lives to discover ourselves:

> Inquiry is basically a matter of participating in the stream, cooperating with the current, going with the flow, in such a way that you are aligning yourself with the optimizing force. (page 156)

When we inquire, we can see whether we are going upstream or downstream. Inquiry work requires that you become your own detective, following clues and analyzing your own motivations until a clear picture of who you are emerges. I urge clients to go up in a virtual helicopter to get a bird's-eye view of who they are and why they act the way they do. Some teachers refer to this as going up in the balcony. Native American elders talk of taking the soaring hawk's view of life.

By pulling back to get perspective, we can go to a witness space from where we can watch ourselves as if on a movie screen. No longer engaged in the heat of our drama, we can see more clearly how our ego and addictive reactions get in the way. With the space provided by pulling back, we realize we can make a decision in each moment to act in the way that best serves us.

Almaas often refers to inquiry work as following a thread. For example, I have a client who realized that she felt emotionally abandoned as a child. She was living with a man who treated her more like a servant than a lover. He was a wealthy, retired doctor yet he expected her, after a hard day of work, to come home and do several hours of chores. She had come to me feeling beaten down and depressed.

As we followed her thread, she realized that she was willing to endure almost anything for love, just so she would not feel abandoned. I asked her to observe how her body felt and what feelings arose when she was talking to him. Soon she realized that when she was with him her belly was tight, contracted, and she felt like a little child. On some level, she believed she could not survive without him. As she watched herself from her witness space, she saw how she was reacting, like a child desperate not to be abandoned again. From this perspective, she saw her choice point was whether she wanted to be in a relationship that required her to give herself up.

As we start to really see ourselves, it empowers us to stretch into our higher selves.

When unfoldment is occurring, the current is more luminous, more radiant, more alive, revealing newer possibilities. The more the current that is our life reveals new possibilities, and the more it becomes creative and unfolds in an optimizing way, the closer we get to our true nature, the pure essence of our Being.

In fact, you might even say that we are then approaching the source of the current. [This] also means that we are approaching the fullness of what we can be. By manifesting our possibilities, by actualizing our potential, by creatively bringing out our further possibilities, we approach our completeness, our wholeness.

—A. H. Almaas, *Spacecruiser Inquiry,* page 157

FOLLOWING A THREAD

Find a thread in your life and follow it. Instead of looking for the "right" thread, just see what arises and value it even if it doesn't seem important enough. Approach it with curiosity and lightness. Avoid trying to "nail" down an answer. Just follow it. Trace it back to when you first remember feeling that way. Take ten minutes to feel into it. Notice how your body feels. What emotions arise? What is your mental activity? Keep in contact with the experience instead of getting into your head. Merely notice what comes up.

Cleaning Your Energy

Self-discovery and self-knowing are vital to mastering the Law of Attraction. Without it, we have lots of static in our energy field repelling what we want and debris attracting what we don't want. Our vibrations are lower because we have old patterns and repressed wounds dragging us down. We unconsciously attract and repeat situations that are more painful because that is what we know.

Repeating patterns is our unconscious way of saying, "This is all I deserve." By looking at our lives, we realize the ways in which we believe we are not worthy. If we follow this long thread of "I am not worthy, I am not enough—smart enough, attractive enough, rich enough . . ." we see how these messages came to us and we can make the decision to believe differently.

> **If you want to change your life—Right Now—there is nothing more powerful than changing what you believe! Belief creates your personal reality: a unique worldview where often what is true is true only for you.**
>
> —Ray Dodd, *The Power of Belief,* page 2

My friend, Susan Glover, a therapist, always asks her clients, "Is there more here?" to expand their experience. For example, if you are sitting on a porch, sharing your heartbreak with supportive friends, you may feel a sense of desolation. Although you don't want to stuff down that feeling or deny it, you ask, "Is there more here?" and widen the area of your feelings. When you look, you can see that, in addition to the heartbreak, you have the support of your friends. If you look further, you can see the trees just off the porch, feel the sun on your back, and smell the freshly cut grass. This allows you to be able to stay with your feelings, yet allow yourself some perspective.

Becoming conscious does not just mean figuring out what has wounded you, what you carry with you, what buttons have been pushed. It means being present in each moment—present to the energy you hold, the static and debris in your field, your emotions, your power—and then making a CONSCIOUS choice as to how you want to experience the moment.

Some may label therapy and other ways of self-knowing as simply gazing at one's navel. Yet to understand ourselves, to engage in

REMOVING SCAR TISSUE

How do you feel about a major wounding? What are the beliefs you have about this wound? How does it stop you from being different? How does it limit you? What are the hidden gifts in the experience?

What are ways you want to rewrite your story? Write a new ending.

inquiry, is an active choice to reclaim our lives because we must go beyond understanding the ways we were wounded. Once we know ourselves, then our challenge is to become free from our story. We can write a new storyline.

Reject a Spiritual Bypass

There are people who believe that, because they are spiritual, they do not need to look at their lives. Teachers refer to this as a spiritual bypass: the belief that by being spiritual we can bypass the process of knowing ourselves because we immediately become enlightened.

Taking a spiritual bypass is merely an excuse to repress or deny parts of ourselves. This is why, sometimes, revered spiritual teachers have dark shadows that sneak out in inappropriate ways such as sexual misconduct, emotional abuse of students, or misuse of money. All of us have heard of ministers, priests, monks, swamis, and lamas who are considered enlightened, yet an ugly story emerges of how they betrayed their followers. Their higher energy centers, the chakras that connect them to God, are open, but they have skipped working on the lower chakras that determine their humanness.

I have had people tell me they no longer have to do any inner work because they are enlightened. Enlightenment is an unfolding process, not a road with only one bridge to cross and then no more travel. Truly enlightened masters know that there is not just one ironclad answer. Enlightenment has no final exam that once you ace, you stop learning. Instead, the more we know, the more we realize how much we don't know and marvel in the mystery of life. Spiritual law is fluid and full of paradox.

Most of us need to live an examined life in order to transcend into higher consciousness.

> **Most teachings actually say, "This is where you're headed, so let's go straight there." This is especially a danger when we become attracted to teachings referred to as sudden, direct, or fast methods. Such approaches might seduce you into believing that you can jump into the [field of] realization without going along with the dynamism itself. The possibility definitely exists that this jump will be successful, but is a minuscule possibility,**

and whether it can happen depends on where you are in your journey.

—A. H. Almaas, *Spacecruiser Inquiry,* page 158

Self-Inquiry Is Not Selfish

There are those who believe that self-inquiry is selfish and self-absorbed. It is true there are some people who make self-examination their only focus. They are driven only by the desire to heal themselves. They often use their wounds as entitlement for their bad behavior. This is not true self-inquiry or they would recognize how their actions hurt themselves and others, and resolve to make other choices.

True self-inquiry is an act of love. When we see our unhealthy patterns, we can move to love. In doing so, we are a gift to others. We learn that not only can we be healed, but we can also be healers. Like a rose unfolding, our soul unfolding is a thing of beauty and a contribution to Earth. Thich Nhat Hanh expresses this in his poem "Kiss the Earth":

Walk and touch peace every moment.
Walk and touch happiness every moment.
Each step brings a fresh breeze.
Each step makes a flower bloom.
Kiss the Earth with your feet.
Bring the Earth your love and happiness.
The Earth will be safe
when we feel safe in ourselves.

Feel Your Feelings

Some spiritual followers even believe they can avoid suffering. They believe that there is no need to feel negative feelings. A priest shared that when his mother died he was dismayed that he felt grief. Since he believed in an afterlife and knew she was in a good place, he felt that he should not experience sadness. He finally realized that grief was a natural process for everyone to work through, even priests. Many teachers of the Law of Attraction counsel us to move quickly from negative emotions to positive emotions. It is true that we must not stay stuck in our negative emotions, but if they arise, we need to experience them before we can move through them.

What feelings are you still repressing? Anything that you repress sneaks out of you in a twisted way to harm others and yourself. If you repress anger, it can creep out as passive aggressiveness or can turn inward as depression. If you repress fear, it can come out with a predator's push or turn you into a control freak.

Clients sometimes ask why they are not attracting what they want. As we talk, I sense that they are filled with fear, even though they deny it. They don't want to feel the fear so they push it down. Often they know that fear will repel what they want most so they won't allow themselves to feel it. But we can't make it go away just because we don't want it. Emotions will linger until we deal with them.

Let your emotions arise strongly in a mindful, meditative process so that they can be released. For example, I urge clients to feel the fear when it comes up. They are expending tremendous energy pushing it down and the unacknowledged fear creates static in their vibration. I ask them to let it fill the room like a cloud and to sit in the fear. The fear grows larger and larger until it is hard to bear. Yet if we stay with it like a spiritual warrior, it starts to dissolve. Soon we feel relief from the fear.

Anger is the same way. I spent years pushing down my anger instead of feeling and expressing it because I didn't feel safe having it. In order not to feel it, I used sadness and grief to cover it over. My spiritual teacher used to tell me that my tears were dampening down the fire of anger that burned deep inside me. When I finally started feeling my anger, I was able to access my strength and change my life.

THE FEELINGS MONSTER

Allow a negative feeling that you have been pushing down to come up. Let it grow. Feel it expand inside of you and then come through the pores of your skin into the room. Give it a color and let it fill the room. Feel how big it is. Don't panic. Sit with it. Just as it feels like it is going to overtake you, it will start to decrease. Stay with the feeling until it dissolves.

Your Life's Work

Inquiry work is indeed work. It is not always fun or pleasant to see how often we are unconscious in our reactions and in acting out old addictive patterns. It can be uncomfortable.

After engaging in self-discovery, it is dismaying to see the same issue resurface again after we believed we had conquered it. It is like rounding the bend in the river to see the same sharp rock looming. We feel like journeyers without a map as we keep walking in circles, destined to stay lost in our own lives.

Take heart on this journey! A map of your life will emerge from the wilderness when you can survey your own homeland like a cartographer.

Lift up the self by the Self
And don't let the self droop down,
For the Self is the self's only friend
And the self is the Self's only foe.

—Bhagavad-Gita 6:5

The Self Is the Self's Only Foe

Sometimes we feel like we *are* our own foe. We wonder why we do this work on ourselves because we keep tripping and falling down. There are times when I put my head in my hands and groan about how I have stumbled into the same hole again.

My first coach had a wonderful story about how we walk down a street and fall in a hole. The next time we walk down the same street and fall in the same hole again. A third time we walk down the same street and fall in a different hole. The fourth time we walk around the holes. The fifth time we walk down a different street.

We all fall down in the same holes repeatedly. This is the drawback of being a huge person-sized magnet! We continue to attract what we most want to change. Yet if we keep working with it, and ask God for help, we can unhook ourselves from our old patterns. Sometimes, however, things get worse before they get better.

Falling Down the Rabbit Hole

I felt like I had fallen down a rabbit hole when I was arrested and had my house go into foreclosure proceedings in the same week. The worst and best things were happening. Right before the crisis, my financial picture was improving and several opportunities had come my way. I had just gotten a blessing and a mantra from the guru Amachi, the Indian "hugging saint." In the middle of the crisis, my children and I had taken a short vacation at a state park cabin where the park director told us we were the first to see an albino deer with her albino fawn. We had a wonderful time.

In addition, my father had offered to pay for my trip if I would accompany him to Peru for a conference. When the conference organizers saw my resume, they asked me to lead two panels in addition to presenting my paper.

A Mixed Bag

Peru was magical. My paper was well received and I made numerous business connections. Conference attendees and taxi drivers stopped me to say I had a beautiful soul and they could feel my heart. Clearly, I was vibrating some positive energy, despite my stay in jail and almost losing my house.

But things were not working so well at home. Although everything had been resolved with my house payments, it was advertised in the local newspaper as being up for public auction. This prompted a stampede of anxiety from all the significant people in my life who knew nothing about the imminent foreclosure.

Each morning, I received hysterical emails from people who loved me and were not sure if I would have a house when I returned. In one week, between being arrested and almost losing my home, I had jeopardized my professional reputation with two of the largest markets that I attract clients from: local government and realtors.

I tried all the centering techniques I knew, I used all the ways to get back into a place of love and joy that is so essential for the Law of Attraction, and I created some wonderful experiences in Peru. But my mojo wasn't reaching home.

A Stampede of Negativity

My third day in Peru, after spending my morning wading through an email barrage, my children, in some convoluted burst of energy back home, knocked over the china cabinet, shattering all my lead crystal but, surprisingly, no one was hurt. The broken debris in my home symbolized the debris cluttering up my energy field.

While my ever-nurturing sister-in-law was calming down my nanny via a phone call, my ex-husband came to pick up one child for some one-on-one time and, discovering the chaos, took them all, without informing the nanny. When she came out a few minutes later to find no children, her immediate fear was they had been kidnapped. She was so distraught over the situation that she moved out early. Bless her heart—she went through a lot in three weeks, too!

Upon my return to a disarrayed home, I discovered that my ex-husband had pulled my youngest daughter, Sophia, who had just turned five, out of preschool. He also registered her for kindergarten without my permission. It was two weeks before school started and all the good preschools were full. I desperately tried to re-enroll her but we had lost the spot and, frankly, the preschool did not want to get in the middle of two fighting parents.

My mother urged me to try the cooperative preschool that my two older children had gone to, but I saw no way that I could do it as a full-time working mom. I called anyway, they were full, and the waiting list was five kids deep.

I spent that day sobbing my heart out. Although I had shed some tears during this whole crisis, the heart-wrenching sobs that overcame me that day felt like they might drown me. I had reached my limit: jail, foreclosure, broken glass and an overturned china cabinet, children disappearing, a distraught nanny moving out, and now this deepest hurt—my baby pushed into school when I strongly felt she wasn't ready.

I went to bed that night feeling like a fallen soldier.

A New Day

I woke the next morning and decided I needed to take my own advice. As one of my coach friends said, I took out MY sword. I shook my finger, yelled, and told the Universe "no more."

Now, I know that if we put focus and energy on the "no," that is what we will get more of. But this was different. Anger is a great emotion to create movement and action. I said it once and it moved me out of my victim space. Then I was able to move forward instead of sinking deeper into the quicksand.

Surrender Is Sweet Victory

I admitted to God that, obviously, I had been trying to control too much in some areas and hadn't exerted enough in others. That I still had wounds that kept me from feeling worthy enough to receive all the good I wanted. And that, clearly, I did not love myself enough.

Then as any twelve-step program will tell you, I gave it up to

God. I said: This is more than I can handle, and obviously, my whole manifestation mojo is not working. I asked for help and assured God I would receive any lifeboat that was sent to me.

God Responds

God responded swiftly. My mother called within an hour saying that she and my stepfather would share the preschool responsibilities so it would not affect my work as much. The preschool registrar called me to say that the most unlikely thing had happened—a family was going to have to move out of state. Because my daughter's older siblings had attended the same preschool, she was moved ahead in the waiting list. And by the way, would I like a scholarship? I almost cried with joy right there on the phone.

Harmony started to prevail. My ex-husband, who had been insistent on Sophia attending kindergarten, invited me over to sit on his porch for a civil negotiation about sending her to preschool.

And little Sophia loved the new preschool so much. I watched her jauntily march in every morning, her little face eager to see her friends. She confided to me that she liked her other preschool but she *looooved* this one.

My life went back to smooth sailing. Work flowed in. My finances regained stability. My house stayed my house. My children thrived. Opportunity after opportunity came to me.

I learned so much about myself in that short crash course. I saw how I needed to master the details in my life, including my financial security. I noticed that I still shut down when I feel overwhelmed and went right into denial. Most important, I realized that on an unconscious level, I still felt like a victim sometimes.

Deep in Your Energy Field

Deep in your energy field, you can have debris that attracts extremely negative experiences even when you are actively practicing the Law of Attraction, as I was. This debris arises from beliefs about your unworthiness and from deeply engrained patterns, and perhaps is even impacted by agreements made before your birth or in past lives.

We will not always know why something is attracted to us. In fact, we must surrender to delusion if we think we can completely understand all the subtleties of spiritual law. Instead, we must work to know ourselves.

Oh Why, Oh Why . . .

I searched for answers so I could learn from my experience. The concrete answers were easy: Pay attention to details and take responsibility for your life. Yet the extreme consequences and the intensity of the experience prompted me to ask why all those disasters occurred in such a short time frame. What spiritual law had I been messing with?

I received guidance but no definitive answer telling me "why" it all happened. The last day of my crisis, my sister-in-law called to tell me she had a dream that I was battling a large demon. Her interpretation was that I was under attack from the Devil, and I agreed that I was fighting off demons, although I suspect they were of my own making.

Finally, I went to a spiritual healer. As she worked on my energy centers, she commented on how clear they were—until she got to my heart chakra. All of a sudden, I felt tremendous physical pain as if someone were stabbing nails into my heart.

I saw a vision of an angry mob of men around me in pointed hats yelling that they wanted me to die. They confiscated my property, took my children, and put me in a room with bars. They told me I was a witch, and they were afraid of my power. I remember thinking, "I'm a healer, not a witch."

Although I am accustomed to visions, I have never experienced anything so intense or something that was physically painful. The healer worked on me and suggested perhaps a past-life regression had occurred.

Until that point, I hadn't thought much about past lives nor fully embraced the concept. Certainly, there were clues that this explanation was plausible. As a child, I was fascinated with stories of the witch trials. As an adult, people would ask me sometimes if I was a witch. In Peru, a conference attendee had told me I was a good witch when I encouraged him to engage in positive thinking. After my divorce, I would occasionally get a note or email from my ex-husband asking me if I was a good witch or a bad witch.

I Have to Worry about Past-Life Debris?

Thrown by this new perspective, I sought counsel. Several people suggested I had recapitulated my crisis from a past life. After all, in a three-week period, I almost lost my property and my children (temporarily), and I had been behind bars.

Others believed that I had attracted the crisis of a past life through the Law of Attraction. I was dismayed to consider that not only did my patterns from this life attract crisis, but I also now had to worry about past lives!

A Hollywood Ending

This story had not yet played itself out, however. Its completion was an ending that should have been written by Hollywood. I still marvel at how incredible it was!

Six weeks later, as I was preparing to take my children to our first Renaissance Faire, I received an email from my ex-husband asking if I was a good witch or a bad witch. In the past, I would simply roll my eyes, but this time it felt spooky.

During the fair, we attended a belly dance performance at the request of my daughter Sophia. As it ended and we were getting ready to leave our seats, we noticed that another show was starting, so we decided to stay. It was a mock witch trial.

The performer asked for a volunteer. I felt moved to raise my hand and soon the whole crowd was chanting, "Pick her, pick the white witch." My kids and I had come in costume and I was wearing a white Renaissance dress.

I went up on stage and was put on trial. The performer passed out scripts to audience members for them to use in accusing me of witchcraft. It was all done for humor and I tried to be playful, although it was hard not to be freaked out by the eeriness of it.

At the end of the show, I was found guilty. The performer asked the audience if they wanted to hang me and they shouted back "no." He asked if they wanted to drown me and they shouted back "no." He asked how they wanted me to die and three hundred people started shouting, "Burn her, burn her, BURN HER!"

He took out a large theatrical match and struck it. An enormous flame jumped up and he held it near me. **And then it went out.**

The mock judge then pronounced, "Oh, it is an act of God. God does not want us to burn an innocent woman today. You are acquitted."

An Act of God

I still cannot say if I created the crisis and its aftermath out of a past-life experience. Or if it was just a metaphor to illuminate my fear of moving into a more public role writing a book about such a magical "woo woo" subject as the Law of Attraction. I don't need to know.

What I do know is that it forced me to examine all the static and debris I carried in my vibration. I literally had to clean up my act. There was no way I ever wanted to live through such an intense experience again.

I did feel acquitted. I lived through the trial unscathed. An act of God had kept things from getting worse and God's hand created a happy ending. I shudder to think about my children placed in foster care while I was arrested or them becoming homeless from losing our house. I am reminded that God can take over my problems and come up with solutions that are far better than what I could have imagined.

Every time I saw my happy little girl getting ready for the pre-school that was perfect for her, I thanked God for Her intervention.

Joy is a great teacher.

So is humor. In the final scene of my Hollywood-like drama, the Universe proved to have quite a sense of humor.

A Creator's Sense of Humor

We can use joy and humor to help us move through a negative experience. Almost always, if we look, we can see the positive. Sometimes also the absurd.

During my rigorous solo mountain hike, I found myself tortured with monkey mind chatter about my old boyfriend. I prayed to God that I could be present and mindful of my surroundings on my hike. I promptly got lost! All of a sudden, I was present and mindful of my surroundings—and stressed out.

When I realized what I had done, I rewrote my prayer. I asked to be joyful and peaceful while I was present and mindful. Soon I found my way back to the trail. Clearly, I was being taught a lesson about being specific! From now on, I include the words "joyful" and "peaceful" in my requests.

Call to Change

By looking for the positive or the absurd, we reframe our perspective on life. We start to change by changing our thought patterns. I urge clients to do this by reframing a negative thought into a positive thought. For instance, when I got lost, I could be angry or frightened by the lesson I was being taught—or I could be amused.

A powerful process arose out of my mountain hike that helped quiet all those negative thoughts that were flying around in my mind like a firestorm and reframe my experience. I call it **The Three**

Power Call for Change Process and it brings about change once your self-inquiry has identified a pattern that is causing you suffering. Through it, you access three different powers depending on how entrenched your negative thought pattern has become. The powers are the call to love, call to action, and call to God.

Call to love. When you first notice the negative thought, remember to bring love into the equation. Whether you are trying to disable the inner critic from criticizing you, to quiet obsessive thoughts, or to change an addictive pattern, ask for love. Remember, these are the ways we are abusive to ourselves. To persist is a form of self-hatred and self-torture. Be kind to yourself and call for love. Focus on the feeling. Feel love come and wash over you.

Call to action. If you continue to struggle after calling for love, then call for action. Break the cycle by taking some form of action. Get up and take a walk. Stop and smell a flower. Dance, sing, run, or jump. Turn on music or call someone and tell a joke. Interrupt your mind by changing focus and moving your body.

Call to God. Sometimes the negative pattern has its claws buried deep in you. Focusing on your feelings and calling in love fails to release it. Moving to action and changing your focus can't dislodge it. Call in your powerful ally. Ask God to banish the demon you battle. Surrender the problem to God.

I teach this three-power process to my clients and many report that they have effectively changed their mind patterns.

THREE POWERS FOR A POWER LIFE

Bring to mind a problem that has been troubling you. Try using **The Three Power Call for Change Process** to neutralize it.

Your Strongest Ally

Whatever your problem, you can move through it with God's help. God can help you change your thought patterns or rescue you from a disaster.

Sometimes it takes us a while to comprehend fully that God is our strongest ally. I thought I had a deep relationship with God, but I really wasn't cocreating with my Creator. I was not fully receiving

God because I was not fully surrendering to God. Once I was able to say, "This problem is bigger than I am," everything changed.

Remember, once more: You don't have to create your life all on your own. You have a cocreation partner! I learned there is an important balance between using the Law of Attraction to create my life and giving it over completely to God to get me out of a jam.

Surrendering to Miracles

You guide me with your counsel, and afterward you [receive] me into glory.

—Psalm 73:24

When I was delivered from my crisis, I told friends it was the Molly Michie Preschool Miracle because that was my turning point—but it really was the Michelle Miracle. Once again, I was reminded that it is not just up to me. Divine intervention can come in and sweep everything away, clear up the debris, and present us with even better solutions than we come up with ourselves.

Our vibrations really do matter, but there are times when what we attract comes from deep in our energy field, until, no matter what we do in the moment, the avalanche starts coming. My feelings of worthiness and self-love needed work, as did a nagging feeling of victimization.

It is at these times that we are reminded we are not alone. We need to see ourselves clearly and we need help from God to overcome our addictive patterns. Those who work with twelve-step programs know this wisdom. Again, we don't have to do this all on our own!

Your Highest Self Is Already There

The teachings of Abraham, through Esther and Jerry Hicks, tell us that our greatest problems come from resisting what our Greater Self has already become.

Your work is to become conscious to your life. In doing so, you catch up to your Highest Self.

God's work is to help you change your life. Your soul triumphs.

The Triumph of the Soul
Joy! Joy! I triumph! Now no more I know

Myself as simply me. I burn with love
Unto myself, and bury me in love.
The centre is within me and its wonder
Lies as a circle everywhere about me.
Joy! Joy! No mortal thought can fathom me.
I am the merchant and the pearl at once.
Lo, Time and Space lie crouching at my feet.
Joy! Joy! When I would reveal in a rapture.
I plunge into myself and all things know.

—Attar

CHAPTER 14

Moving from Doing to Being

I sat on my meditation rock, the one that overlooks two streams as they converge. Something had changed in me. The quiet, the prayer, the contemplation, the conversations with God—all had produced a shift. Time stood still.

I felt bliss rise up in my body and God's hand on my shoulder. My energy felt clean, whole, and loving. I gave thanks. I was completely at peace.

Then I stood up, asked for the grace to be able to carry this space with me, and returned to my busy, hectic life.

And the bliss did not fade, nor the peace that came with it. I carried it with me into a life that was more easeful and flowing.

Call a new life. Welcome bliss. Summon peace. Reach toward love in every moment. Release resentments and old wounds.

Ask for ease and grace in your life. Cultivate gratitude for all you have and all you wish to have. Include God in every equation. Request guidance. Cocreate your life. Ride the flow of your river current.

You have invited God fully into your life. You have embraced the Law of Attraction. You are working on dissolving resistance to accepting gifts. You have taken back your power and claimed responsibility for your life. You are working to be a conscious person who is self-aware and mindful of the choices you are making and the energy you hold.

You receive yourself, your higher guidance, and God's love.

Now it is time to remember to *be*.

Sounds paradoxical, doesn't it? Most of this book has been about what you can DO to invite God in and cocreate your life. Now you are being asked to merely BE.

Being is the energy we hold. Being is when we let things move through us. Being is how we vibrate. Being is the gift we give others and ourselves.

> **If you choose peace and joy and love, you won't get much of it through what you're doing. If you choose happiness and contentment, you'll find little of that on the path of doingness. If you choose reunion with God, supreme knowing, deep understanding, endless compassion, total awareness, absolute fulfillment, you won't achieve much of that out of what you're doing. . . . *Doing* is a function of the body. *Being* is a function of the soul.**
>
> —Neale Donald Walsch, *Conversations with God, Book 1,* page 170

Being Is from the Soul

Being is the very essence of the soul and it celebrates connection. When we are "being," we understand, on the soul level, that everything is connected. The Taoist book of wisdom, the *Tao Te Ching,* praises this quality and compares it to the fluidness of water. It urges us to "do without 'doing.'"

Taoists believe the path of "action through inaction," *wu-wei,* is superior. The Asian notion of *wu-wei* has been greatly misunderstood because of translation and Western resistance to the word "inaction." Instead of being passive, *wu-wei* means intuitive cooperation with the natural order and the belief that everything is perfect and harmonious.

When we can come from the perspective that everything is perfect and harmonious, our suffering over how we think people and things "should" be ends. We stop wading upstream in our river. Instead, we turn and go with the flow. We do not consume our energy with trying to figure out why something happened. Instead, when we regard everything as perfect, our question becomes "What do I need to learn from this?"

Bryon Katie challenges us in her book *Loving What Is* to look at everything we suffer about with the question "Is this true—do I really know this is true?" This simple process that she calls "The Work" forces us to see how much of our suffering is because we think things "should" be different. As we move to accept how things are, we free up our energy to enjoy our life as it is and cocreate what we want. In other words, we turn our boat to go with the current.

"Shoulds" Drag Us Down

When we want something so badly, whether a deeper relationship with God, a life partner, a child, or monetary success, we can repel it from us by a desperate clinging to the want. We become attached to how it "should" come or on what schedule it "must" come. "Should" is a word we use to reject our life experiences or ourselves. It is a guaranteed way to create suffering in our lives and lower our vibrations. "Shoulds" drag us down or even push away what we want most.

Buddha reminds us that all suffering comes from attachment. Attachment has a rigid, controlling quality, very unlike the fluidity of visioning a want and receiving it. When we believe that our life "should" be different, instead of being able to create how we want it to be different, we remain as victims. We push against what we have, so we have no room to receive what we want. Then we bemoan that we never get what we want. It is a vicious cycle.

Attachment is wading upstream, fighting the current with every step and trying to force an outcome. Like the Chinese students I spoke to, it is thinking that success comes from working even harder and pushing ourselves further.

> **We've been taught that we gain only as we labor, that action is the magic word. Do, do, do; work, work, work, strive, sweat, toil, and then if our luck holds, we just might come out ahead.**
>
> —Lynn Grabhorn, *Excuse Me, Your Life Is Waiting*, page 6

"Doing" the Law of Attraction

When people first learn about the Law of Attraction, they want to know how to "do it right." If they are unsuccessful in attracting what they want, they want to know what they need to "do."

Although taking action demonstrates to God that we are serious about what we want, what is more important is the energy we hold so we can let it in. The *Tao Te Ching* accurately describes the energy necessary to receive blessings by urging "action through inaction."¹ As Zen master Seng-ts'an says, "The perfect way is without difficulty."

The perfect way is shown to us through synchronicity. In fact, when the path is smoothed for us and all things line up so that we feel we are in a state of grace, it is an indication we are being given Divine guidance to proceed.

If the same negative pattern keeps occurring, it is a sign that we have a life lesson we have not yet learned. Life stops flowing just as a blocked stream does.

Challenges provide us with an opportunity. We can assess whether we are going in the right direction or examine what we must learn. Then we align ourselves so that we can receive what we want. As we align ourselves, we sink more into our "being."

Upon learning a lesson, we are given a few tests to assure that we have "be-come" new. Again, this too must be approached in a loving and contemplative manner, without a striving to "make it right" (an energy I know much about!).

Joyful Playfulness

Remember how to play. As a child, you were at your best when you were playing. Joy arose naturally. Approach the creation of your life with this same energy. When you decide to ride the river downstream, you can only catch the current if you fill your boat with joy and playfulness. To set your jaw with determination and work hard at going downstream, so that you can succeed at creating, really means you are just finding another way to paddle your little boat upstream again.

Joy and playfulness come from enjoying the process and playing with it like you might play in the river on your journey. Playing enhances success and ensures the journey is as pleasurable as the destination. Timothy Gallwey, who wrote *The Inner Game of Tennis,* *The Inner Game of Golf,* and *The Inner Game of Work,* was one of the first life and work "coaches." As he taught tennis and golf, he discovered that the more his students learned techniques about how they "should" hit the ball, the worse they got. When he got them out of their heads, added an element of play in it so they enjoyed themselves, and asked them to "feel" hitting the ball on a gut level, their games improved.

Lynn Grabhorn exhorts us to "feeeeeel" our wants into existence. Take this advice and go further with it. "Feeeeel" your "being" into existence. As you move into being, you no longer live a life conditional on outside factors. You thrive and grow regardless of the soil you are planted in or the water you receive. As you thrive, your outside world starts to mirror your inside world.

Dancing through Life

When we dance with joy, we are both doing and being. As a passionate dancer, I love the image of dancing through life. Philosopher Alan Watts posed this provocative dilemma to us. He observed that many people think the purpose of life is a race. They race through life from one goal to another, yet as they get to the finish line, they realize it is not a race they want to win. It dawns on them that the end is death and the point of life was in the journey.

Watts asked us instead to consider life as a dance or as music. In both, the magic is in the process, not in rushing toward a finish line. Consider how different dancing is from racing. One dances until the music is finished. The purpose is in the beauty of the dance and in how it makes us feel. Dancing is a process filled with joy, playfulness, and passion. What if we were to live our lives this way?

Music, dancing, rhythm—all these are art forms which have no goal other than themselves, and to participate in them fully is to lay aside all thought of a necessary future; to say "must" to a rhythm is to stop it dead. In the moment when he is anxious to play the correct notes, the musician is blocked. In both senses, he stops playing. He can only perfect his art by continuing to play, practicing without trying until the moment comes when he finds that correct rhythm plays itself.

All perfect accomplishment in art or life is accompanied by the curious sensation that it is happening of itself— that it is not forced, studied or contrived.

—Alan Watts, *Psychotherapy, East and West,* pages 211–212

Although dancing or music is something we DO, when we are immersed in the process, it also is something we ARE. Thus even in the doing, we are being.

Dancing with God

By making every action a prayer to God, we become what we are trying to do. We receive grace in our everyday lives. Spirit leads us.

Leap into a life of love. Allow yourself to be led by God. Feel the bliss of the dance.

I cannot dance, Lord, unless you lead me.
If you want me to leap with abandon,
You must intone the song.
Then I shall leap into love,
From love into knowledge,
From knowledge into enjoyment,
And from enjoyment beyond all human sensations.
There I want to remain, yet want also to circle higher still.

—St. John of the Cross

Being Is a Choice

The invocation that starts out the *The Book of Runes* reminds us of this:

God within me, God without,
How shall I ever be in doubt?
There is no place where I may go
And not there see God's face, not know. . . .
So through the harvest of my years
I am the sower and the Sown,
God's self unfolding and God's own.

Remember we are the sower and the sown. What we sow, we reap. Sowing and reaping goes beyond what we want in life. When we can become mindful, conscious people who choose love and peace as the energy we hold, we sow love and peace. Our energy is a gift to the world and what we do ripples out through the Universe.

Buddhists believe in sending loving-kindness to all sentient beings. They have meditation practices focused on developing compassion. They understand that cultivating compassion and loving-kindness is even more powerful than giving a handout to those in need. They see the correlation to the healing power of their energy.

Native Americans instruct us to remember "all our relations." They stress their concept of the "giveaway" where you give without regard to what you get back. When you cultivate the energy of love, you are living the space of the "giveaway."

We can't fix a broken world by ourselves, yet when we live in the world this way, we bless many people. For those who choose to work for social justice or peace or the environment, their loving-kindness energy will impact the outcome in a way an angry organizer's "doing" cannot.

Your Outer Life will begin to reflect your Inner Reality about Who You Are and Who You Choose to Be.

—Neale Donald Walsch, *Bringers of the Light*, page 67

You can produce a State of Being by simply selecting one. And you can do this anytime, anywhere. A State of Being is a feeling, not an action. You can undertake to feel a certain way. That is, you have the power to decide how you're going to feel, and how you feel right now.

—Neale Donald Walsch, *Bringers of the Light*, page 42

Let Go, Let God

Inherent in the joy and pleasure of creating is accepting our oneness with God. When we remember our unity, we can receive ourselves because we are part of God. We also can trust that God will provide for us. We don't need to micromanage what happens or how it shows up. We just need to ask and receive.

Repeatedly in my conversations with God, I am told, "Supports will be given." When I express fear, I am asked, "Have I not always provided for you?"

Receiving that God will provide for us and loves us unconditionally means we are fully receiving God's love and accepting that we are worthy. Not only are we choosing love over fear, but we are also allowing bliss instead of sorrow.

When I listen to God, this is what I hear:

I receive everyone. You came to me because you felt weak with hunger. You needed to drink the elixir of love. You wanted to feel it intensely because what you had drunk before that was called love was like a cheap wine that left you thirsty and bitter. You know, despite your experiences, that love must have sweetness to it.

Nothing tastes sweeter than the elixir of love from God. It is our manna from heaven. It gives rise to bliss. Do not be afraid to indulge in it even if life has tasted sour in the past. When we eat from this bread and drink from this cup, our life is filled in a way we never knew possible.

Loving Yourself

Allowing Who You Really Are to arise is the ultimate form of self-love.

> **The philosophy of wu-wui or noninterference implies . . . the apparently dangerous counsel that people must accept themselves as they are. This will disturb the social order far less than splitting themselves apart to strive after impossible ideals.**
>
> —Alan Watts, *Psychotherapy, East and West,* page 88

For years, my spiritual teacher Deane Shank has counseled me that the most compassionate thing I can do for others is to show up in life as me. He cautions, "When we put a direction on who we are, we already put a separation between *who we believe we are* and *who we really are.*"

When we accept ourselves—when we receive our souls—we no longer have to strive. We can sink into our hearts and operate from the heart's depths. In Zen terminology, the liberated man has "no mind," a place called *wu-hsin.* This concept of "no mind" comes from feeling our divinity and living from our hearts. This wise place of being, named *summum bonum* (Latin for "the true end of man"), occurs when we live in our highest good.

The Turning Point Is the Pleasure in the Being

Diamond Approach Work teaches that when we can feel pleasure in our "being," we have made a huge leap in our spiritual development. Relaxing into the pleasure of our "being" means we accept and feel value in ourselves. If we feel our value, then what we do has value. We bring value to our daily actions and all in our lives feel our loving presence. We live a life from inside out, not outside in.

Value has a tremendous impact on our ability to "be" our self. Are we trying to get value for ourselves from the outside? A lot of suffering comes from having things we value that don't have value.

Understanding how we create this suffering for ourselves is a huge step to becoming conscious. Deane teaches that if we don't value the truth, we don't value who we are. Our search, to know who and what we are, takes us to the depths of our souls.

The human soul is lost, estranged from its home. We were home once but now we can't find our way back. We have a sense of returning home when we feel our value. Each time we reach a little deeper, there is a realization: I'm closer to home. Joy and excitement arise with each step.

—Deane Shank

Our soul wants to know itself by feeling who we are, by sensing who we are, by BEING who we are. Thus by knowing ourselves, we know God. And who we are is part of God. As Zen Master Hakuin says: "This very earth is the Lotus Land of purity. And this very body the Body of Buddha." Perfection is here in us. Heaven is here in our lives. Rapture is here now. We cocreate it with God in each moment.

A River of Grace

Heaven is here! It lives in the gifts we can choose to request and receive. It exists inside of us and when we can distinguish it in our inner lives, then it starts to show up in our outer lives.

After fighting a rough river and being pounded into rocks, I finally see this. Even during the toughest periods of my life, heaven lived within reach inside me. Although there were times after my child's death and during my divorce when my life felt like a scorched landscape, a lush garden was growing inside me watered by a river of grace. Without those experiences, I would not be who I really am. I am so grateful for my life—both the joy and the pain. And now I know that I can make the choice to receive more joy than pain. I can choose to channel grace moment by moment. Every second gives me a new chance for a new life.

When I left the solitude of the cabin for the last time, I reintegrated into my life. People asked me what I was doing differently. They said I felt solid and grounded. Some commented that I looked more girlish. What I knew was that my energy was different. I could feel myself in my skin. I felt centered and spacious. I felt both more solid and lighter. I had surrendered, yet felt more powerful.

What I finally realized is that I float in a river of grace and it has always been there, accessible to me even as I fought the rapids. Sometimes I even feel I AM the river.

Baptism in the River

Your river of life is your creation. You and God have cocreated it so that your soul can fully experience life. You came to ride the river and to BE the river.

> *See, the streams of living waters,*
> *springing from eternal love,*
> *well supply thy sons and daughters,*
> *and all fear of want remove.*
> *Who can faint while such a river*
> *ever will their thirst assuage?*
> *Grace which like the Lord, the giver,*
> *never fails from age to age.*
>
> —John Newton, "Glorious Things of Thee Are Spoken"

Do not underestimate the power of being love. Like water, there is force and power in it. Water wears grooves into granite rocks and creates deep riverbeds. By making different choices, you establish new pathways in your brain and retrain your neural pathways to receive a life of love. Your heart's jagged places will be worn smooth like a river rock. God's love can wash away darkness and negativity so that your soul fills with light.

Baptize yourself in your river. Renew yourself with your Source. You may have come to God to be healed. Now it is time to be the healer. Become healing waters to those around you. Move from healing to "be-coming" a healer just by the energetic space you hold in this world.

Do not take this journey just for yourself. Take the journey for all of us.

Turn your little boat and ride the river of grace.

I leave you with this blessing:

> *Row, Row, Row your boat*
> *Gently down the stream.*
> *Merrily, Merrily, Merrily, Merrily,*
> *Life is but a dream.*

Resources

Almaas, A. H. *Spacecruiser Inquiry: True Guidance for the Inner Journey*. Boston: Shambhala, 2002.

Buddhist Promoting Foundation, *The Teaching of Buddha*. Tokyo: Kosaido Printing, 1966.

Byrne, Rhonda. *The Secret*. New York: Atria Books, 2006.

Covington, Dennis. *Salvation on Sand Mountain: Snake Handling and Redemption in Southern Appalachia*. Reading, MA: Addison-Wesley, 1995.

Dodd, Ray. *The Power of Belief*. Boulder, CO: Mount Baldy Press, 2004.

Dyer, Wayne W. *The Power of Intention*. Carlsbad, CA: Hay House, 2004.

———. *Real Magic*. New York: HarperCollins, 1992.

Fox, Matthew. *Original Blessing*. New York: Jeremy P. Tarcher/Putnam, 2000.

Gaines, Edwene. *The Four Spiritual Laws of Prosperity: A Simple Guide to Unlimited Abundance*. New York: Rodale, 2005.

Gallwey, Timothy. *The Inner Game of Work*. New York: Random House, 2000.

Gilbert, Elizabeth. *Eat, Pray, Love*. New York: Viking, 2006.

Grabhorn, Lynn. *Excuse Me, Your Life Is Waiting*. Charlottesville, VA: Hampton Roads, 2000.

———. *The "Excuse Me, Your Life Is Waiting" Playbook*. Charlottesville, VA: Hampton Roads, 2001.

Hanh, Thich Nhat. *Living Christ, Living Buddha*. New York: Riverhead, 2007.

Hay, Louise. *You Can Heal Your Life*. Santa Monica, CA: Hay House, 1987.

Hicks, Esther, and Jerry Hicks. *The Amazing Power of Deliberate Intent*. Carlsbad, CA: Hay House, 2006.

———. *Ask and It Is Given*. Carlsbad, CA: Hay House, 2004.

Ingerman, Sandra. *Shamanic Journeying: A Beginner's Guide*. Louisville, CO: Sounds True, 2004.

————. *Soul Retrieval: Mending the Fragmented Self.* San Francisco: HarperSanFransisco, 1991.

Katie, Byron. *Loving What Is.* New York: Harmony Books, 2002.

Kornfield, Jack. *After the Ecstasy, the Laundry.* New York: Bantam, 2000.

————. *A Path with Heart.* New York: Bantam, 1993.

Kushner, Harold S. *When Bad Things Happen to Good People.* New York: Schocken Books, 1989.

Lerner, Gerda. *The Creation of Feminist Consciousness.* New York: Oxford University Press, 1993.

Levine, Stephen. *Guided Meditations, Explorations, and Healings.* New York: Anchor Books, 1991.

Myss, Caroline M. *Entering the Castle.* New York: Free Press, 2007.

————. *Sacred Contracts.* New York: Harmony Books, 2001.

Nemeth, Maria. *The Energy of Money: A Spiritual Guide to Financial and Personal Fulfillment.* New York: Ballantine Books, 2000.

Peale, Norman Vincent. *The Power of Positive Thinking.* New York: Fawcett Columbine, 1996.

Pearson, Carol. *The Hero Within.* San Francisco, CA: HarperSanFrancisco, 1998.

Perry, John Weir. *Lord of the Four Quarters.* New York: Paulist Press, 1991.

Prophet, Elizabeth Clare. *Violet Flame to Heal Body, Mind, and Soul.* Corwin Springs, MT: Summit University Press, 1997.

Smith, Stretton. *Stretton Smith's 4T Prosperity Program.* Carmel, CA: The 4T Publishing Company, 1998.

Tipping, Colin C. *Radical Forgiveness.* Marietta, GA: Global 13 Publishers, 2000.

de Vitray-Meyerovitch, Eva. *Rumi and Sufism.* Trans. Simone Fattal. Sausalito, CA: Post-Apollo Press, 1987.

Walsch, Neale Donald. *Bringers of the Light.* Charlottesville, VA: Hampton Roads, 2000.

————. *Conversations with God, Book 1.* New York: Putnam Publishing Group, 1996.

————. *Conversations with God, Book 2.* Charlottesville, VA: Hampton Roads, 1997.

Watts, Alan. *Psychotherapy, East and West.* New York: Vintage Books, 1975.

Williamson, Marianne. *A Return to Love.* New York: HarperCollins, 1996.

In addition to the books listed above, here are some specific websites organized by subjects mentioned in the book.

Archetypes

Shadow Work Workshops

Shadow Work (www.shadowwork.com) includes a set of facilitated processes that allow individuals to explore and change almost any behavior pattern. Based on Cliff Barry's unique synthesis of ancient and modern tools, Shadow Work uses a four-directional archetypal "map of the mind" to identify and process your "shadows."

Shadow Work Facilitators

Chrissy and Dave McFarren (www.full-circle-farm.net or dave@mcfarren.net).

Belief Changing

Energy Focus Coaching

Coaching by Michelle Prosser (energyfocuscoaching.com).

Spiritual Workshops

Diamond Approach

The Diamond Approach is the spiritual teaching, the path, and the method of the Ridhwan School (www.ridhwan.org). The Ridhwan Foundation is the nonprofit spiritual organization established to support and preserve the integrity of the Diamond Approach teaching.

The Diamond Approach teacher mentioned in book is Deane Shank. To find a teacher, go to www.ridhwan.org/school/teachers.html.

To find Diamond Approach books by founder A. H. Almaas on the Soul, Presence, Essence, and True Nature, go to: www.ahalmaas.com/Books/index.htm.

Meditation

To find Samedya guided meditations (heart energy) created by Sheila Foster, go to www.templeofthesacredfemenine.com. The Samedya meditation teacher mentioned in book is Linda Kolker at www.sylph.com.

Orienteering

To find orienteering teambuilding workshops for office teams, go to www.energyfocuscoaching.com; for orienteering clinics on horseback, visit Olin Bare at www.horsecenter.org.

Shamanism

The Shamanism teacher mentioned in book is Sue Wolfstar. See her website at www.susanwolfstar.com.

Acknowledgments

By now, you know my life is filled with rivers. Fortunately, many river guides have led me down the rivers, more than I can thank here. While I was mired in despair at the end of my marriage, my spiritual teacher Deane Shanks kept me steady. Once as I meditated with him, I saw a vision of myself drowning in a rushing river, swollen with my own tears. Just as panic overtook me, a giant sea turtle appeared and carried me on his back. Surprised, I realized the turtle represented both Deane and my father, my sea turtle totems. Over the years, Deane's solid presence, spiritual guidance, and compassion helped me immeasurably. The generous emotional and financial support of my darling father, Dr. Michael Prosser, kept my head above the water. He also served as an early editor for this book.

Now when I see a sea turtle, it represents mature, wise, male energy for me. Another sea turtle is my coach Russ Long, who coached me (even when I had no funds to pay him) to break lifelong, destructive patterns and to achieve my goals.

Not all river guides swim in the water; some have a bird's eye view above the river. When I struggled to find equilibrium through solitude at the convent grounds, an owl watched over me from less than ten feet away. It felt like a wise woman blessing me and now when I see owls, I think of mature, wise, female energy.

My life overflows with wise women, my blessing owls, as diverse as Sister Louise, my shamanism teacher Sue Wolfstar, and Shadow Work workshop leader Chrissy McFarren (and her husband Dave McFarren). I feel so grateful to my wonderful friends Sandy Ackers, Claudette Borgersen, Ann Karima Gallant, Dana Wassenaar, Tracey Linkous, Suzanne Henry, and Cecelia Haynie (and too many others to name), and to my coach friends Judith Minter, Erin Johnson, Claire Goodman, Lori Nicolaysen, and Smokie Sizemore. Special thanks to my lawyer, Cheryl Higgins, who kept me and many other women safe from domestic abuse and now serves as a judge.

My mother Carol Hill is responsible for much of my early spiritual training. A devout Catholic, she taught me how to pray and to respect all spiritual paths, especially Native American culture and tradition. My mother and her husband Jim Hill (another sea turtle and a Blackfoot Indian) have helped me with my children, and the upkeep of my home.

My children Darya, Sanders, and Sophia did all they could to help their mom complete this book, from playing quietly as I wrote to not complaining about all the extra babysitters. My children shared their spiritual wisdom with me and Darya even helped brainstorm a subtitle. They are extraordinary and I am honored to parent them. My brothers and their wives are raising wise spiritual children and this has been a gift in my family's life. Special mention goes to my sister-in-law Hope Prosser for her spiritual commitment, wise insight, loving friendship and unwavering support.

Families can also be chosen, and I am grateful for the communities of Charlottesville Unity Church and its ministers Reverend Don Lansky and Reverend Patricia Gulino Lansky, the Diamond Approach members, and Molly Michie Preschool.

While I was writing I met a new river guide who been instrumental in the direction of this book. Olin Bare offered me his cabin and then his heart. Without the retreat, this book would not have been finished in the short time-line I was given. An orienteer who takes a long view, Olin has become my North Star. His wise counsel, gentle love, consistent support, and complete acceptance and adoration of me have been one of the greatest gifts I have ever received.

A Course in Miracles teaches that all relationships are eternal on the spiritual plain even if we end them. Our toughest relationships are our greatest teachers. My ex-husband has been a great teacher for me. Although our way was often hard, there were some very beautiful times. I am grateful for our amazing children, especially that he agreed to have them such a fast pace. Although this book contains some negative images of him, he was doing his best at the time and we have both grown from the experience. I share responsibility for being demanding and sometimes controlling in the marriage. I was deeply torn about whether to reveal what happened in our marriage as I did not want to hurt him but ultimately I decided it is my truth and important for me to speak. He is a committed father, a brilliant writer, and his career has flourished since our divorce. I wish him the very best.

Many thanks to Paul Seaman for all he taught me and the gifts he gave me, including our mutual love of swords. He exposed me to teachings about archetypes, Shadow Work workshops, and Native American sweat lodges;

I have so much gratitude for yet another wise woman, my editor Valerie Waterson, who signed on to help me with enthusiasm and energy, kept me on track, and devoted hundreds of hours to the project. Valerie is a superb writer in her own right. Many thanks to Cindy Jennings whose clarity and vision for the book was invaluable in her role as final editor and project manager.

My gratitude to the folks at Hampton Roads Publishing, especially CEO Jack Jennings who "discovered" me; publicist and dear friend Sara Sgarlat, who works tirelessly; Greg Brandenburg, marketing director, who in his infinite wisdom created a new subtitle and stunning cover, and to my ever-patient production manager Jane Hagaman. Special thanks goes to John St.Augustine for sharing his compelling story in the foreword and adding his wisdom and insight to this book.

I would be remiss if I did not acknowledge the many teachers who have influenced and inspired me: Stephen Levine, Alan Watts, Joseph Campbell, Marianne Williamson, Louise Hay, Wayne Dyers, Carolyn Myss, Thomas Merton, Rumi, Ester and Jerry Hicks, Reverend Stratton Smith, Edwene Gains, Neal Donald Walsch, and Lynn Grabhorn. Their teachings have become so engrained in my thinking that it is hard to tease out their ideas and give them credit although I have endeavored to do so.

Thank you all.

About the Author

Michelle Epiphany Prosser, president of Energy Focus Coaching and Consulting, works with organizations and individuals to reach goals and manifest a better life. She is committed to deepening her spirituality and increasing self-awareness so that she can model to clients what she teaches.

She holds an MA in communication studies from the University of Virginia, and certification in a communications styles assessment and life purpose process, and is a trained coach through Success Unlimited Network and Corporate Coach U International.

Michelle's emphasis is on increasing focus and energy, improving communication, and identifying self-defeating behavior. Her gentle coaching style is based on the belief that her clients have most of the answers inside. She helps clients design systems to support their success and to disable their inner critic.

Before becoming a coach, Michelle worked for twenty years in government and politics, including leadership positions for three Virginia governors and a congressman.

She has coached, taught, and worked with senior executives, governors, cabinet secretaries, congressmen, college presidents, and small business owners. In addition to helping them reach their goals, she has prepared them for major speeches, political debates, and national television appearances.

Michelle is frequently interviewed by the media on setting goals and creating the life you want. Her message is we live the life we want not by DOING but by BEING. It is not what we do in life, but the energy we hold while we do it, that determines our success in life.

Michelle Prosser is currently writing her next book, and is collecting stories from people who recovered from crisis and created a happier way to live through spirituality, the Law of Attraction, and self-discovery. If you have a story to share please email her at: energyfocuscoaching@gmail.com.

The Excuse Me, Your Life Is Waiting *Playbook*

With the Twelve Tenets of Awakening

Lynn Grabhorn

Human beings have evolved physically, socially, and technologically, but are unable to take the next step toward spiritual evolution because of self-defeating habits and conditioning—in short, we are our own victims. Lynn Grabhorn has taken the concepts that made *Excuse Me, Your Life Is Waiting* a bestseller and transformed them into a complete workbook for empowerment. The clearly focused explanations, discussion material, meditations, and exercises are essential building blocks to a new way of being. Isn't it worth a little work to have the life you've always wanted?

- Based on the principles of the self-help sensation *Excuse Me, Your Life Is Waiting*
- Ideal for group or individual study
- Crosses the boundaries of age, gender, race, income, and religious belief
- A straight-shooting, carefully orchestrated program for self-improvement

Paperback • 288 pages
ISBN 978-1-57174-270-4 • $22.95

www.hrpub.com • 1-800-766-8009

Excuse Me, Your Life Is Now

Mastering the Law of Attraction

Doreen Banaszak

Lynn Grabhorn's wildly popular book, *Excuse Me, Your Life Is Waiting,* offered four fundamental principles for attracting what we desire most in life. Now Doreen Banaszak has created a sequel that not only presents a convenient review of Grabhorn's four basic tenets—identifying what we don't want, naming what we do want, getting into the feeling of what we want and, finally, allowing what we want to flow into our lives—but also offers overwhelming evidence that these principles really work!

Following Grabhorn's untimely death in 2004, Banaszak, who teaches the principles and has been inundated with true stories of transformation by Grabhorn's readers, assembled this fascinating collection of personal accounts of the principles in practice. These true stories explore the amazing ways that readers' lives have been transformed as these focused, highly motivated individuals put the principles to work to manifest their dreams. As they "got in touch with their feelings," they successfully replaced negative ones like fear, anxiety, and doubt with positive ones like joy, excitement, anticipation, and gratitude. This process allowed their dreams to manifest with astounding speed and clarity! These transformative tales are packed with irrefutable evidence of our magical power to create the life we desire—and detailed instructions on how to do it.

Paperback • 216 pages
ISBN 978-1-57174-543-9 • $15.95

www.hrpub.com • 1-800-766-8009

HAMPTON ROADS
PUBLISHING COMPANY, INC.

Thank you for reading *Excuse Me, Your God Is Waiting*. Hampton Roads is proud to publish a number of books inspired by the Law of Attraction. Please take a look at the following selections or visit us at any time on the web: wwww.hrpub.com.

Excuse Me, Your Soul Mate Is Waiting

Marla Martenson

"Enjoy this book . . . and let it help you find your own soul mate!"
— John Gray, PhD, author of *Men Are from Mars, Women Are from Venus*

Excuse Me, Your Soul Mate Is Waiting

Name what you want.
Feel what you want.
Allow it to happen.

Marla Martenson

". . . a truly unique and important book on the best possible way to find the love of your life."
— Ellen Fein and Sherrie Schneider, coauthors of *All the Rules*

Your lonely days are over. There is someone out there for you, and you can find that person through the Law of Attraction—and keep him or her attracted to you through simple dating rules laid out by Beverly Hills matchmaker Marla Martenson.

With a fun, up-beat tone, reading *Excuse Me, Your Soul Mate Is Waiting* is like getting advice from your best friend—if your friend is an irreverent, sexy matchmaker who is your personal cheerleader and wingman.

Paperback • 200 pages
ISBN 978-1-57174-560-6 • $15.95

www.hrpub.com • 1-800-766-8009

Excuse Me, Your Life Is Waiting

The Astonishing Power of Feelings

Lynn Grabhorn

Ready to get what you want? Half a million readers have answered with an enthusiastic "yes" and have embraced Lynn's principles for achieving the life of their dreams. This upbeat yet down-to-earth book reveals how our true feelings work to "magnetize" and create the reality we experience. Part coach, part cheerleader, Lynn lays out the nuts and bolts of harnessing the raw power of your feelings. Once you becomes aware of what you're feeling, you'll turn the negatives into positives and literally draw all those good things to you like a magnet, creating the life you know you were meant to have—right now!

Discover the secrets that have made *Excuse Me* a *New York Times* bestseller!

Paperback • 328 pages
ISBN 978-1-57174-381-7 • $16.95

www.hrpub.com • 1-800-766-8009